# THE SCOTIA
# WIDOWS

ALSO BY GERALD M. STERN

*The Buffalo Creek Disaster*

# THE SCOTIA WIDOWS

## Inside Their Lawsuit
## Against Big Daddy Coal

· · · · · ·

# Gerald M. Stern

RANDOM HOUSE

NEW YORK

Published in the United States by Random House,
an imprint of The Random House Publishing Group,
a division of Random House, Inc., New York.

RANDOM HOUSE and colophon are registered
trademarks of Random House, Inc.

Grateful acknowledgment is made to the United Mine Workers
of America for permission to reprint the poem entitled "Scotia"
by Harold Shaffer, which appeared in *United Mine Workers Journal,*
April 1–15, 1976. Reprinted by permission.

Library of Congress Cataloging-in-Publication Data
Stern, Gerald M.
The Scotia widows : inside their lawsuit against big daddy coal /
Gerald M. Stern.
p.   cm.
ISBN 978-1-4000-6764-0
1. Blue Diamond Coal Company—Trials, litigation, etc.
2. Trials—Kentucky—Letcher County.   3. Mine explosions—
Kentucky—Letcher County.   I. Title.
KF226.S74 2008
344.7304'65—dc22          2008000071

Printed in the United States of America on acid-free paper

www.atrandom.com

2 4 6 8 9 7 5 3 1

First Edition

Book design by Victoria Wong

*For Jennifer Boggs, Carol Combs, Geraldine Coots,*
*Vera Galloway, Libby Gibbs, Madonna Griffith,*
*Diana McKnight, Geraldine McKnight, Phyllis Peavy,*
*Vickie Scott, Celinda Sparkman, Ethel Sturgill,*
*Debbie Turner, Reda Turner, Charlotte Widner,*
*and their husbands and children.*
*And for my wife, Linda, and our children,*
*Eric, Jesse, and Maia.*

## SCOTIA

Death's rattle rings hard and deep
But passes in a moment's time,
Except for those behind who weep
More murders by another mine.

Today's tragedy of the mining men
Will briefly control the media space:
Tomorrow the memory will be dim
And Scotia a forgotten place.

Layland, Eccles, Hominy Falls—
Just names to blot out.
Too little done about their cause,
Too few to stand and shout.

I wonder how many more must die
Before we hear the mountains' cry.

—HAROLD SHAFFER, whose grandfather
was killed in the Layland, West Virginia,
coal mine disaster of 1915; reprinted from
*United Mine Workers Journal,* April 1–15, 1976

# Prologue

Just before noon on a cold and cloudy day in the Appalachian coal fields of Eastern Kentucky near Oven Fork in Letcher County, on the Poor Fork of the Cumberland River, the Scotia coal mine exploded. The day shift that morning had a crew of 106 men, working six sections of the mine. Almost all of them quickly escaped from the mine after the explosion. But fifteen men, last known to have been working in the Two Southeast Mains section, three and one half miles underground, were unaccounted for. They were young men, most still in their twenties.

A coal mine explosion was not then, and still is not, an uncommon event for coal miners and their families. But the Scotia mine explosion would be different, changing the lives of fifteen young women forever. As the *Philadelphia Inquirer* put it:

> They were local girls, fifteen of them, who had married local boys in that beautiful and blighted

corner of the world called Appalachia. They lived in trailers and frame row houses in coal country, where poor folks still pile coal in the yard as they wait for winter to whirl down the hills. They did not know one another, although their husbands worked the smoldering Scotia Coal mine at Oven Fork. But coal paid the freight in their lives, put cornbread on their tables, and put sooty minstrel faces on their men as they left the mine each day. And coal would thrust the women together, make them lasting friends for life in a way they never dreamed. It would make them coal widows when the Scotia mine blew on the dank, gray morning of March 9, 1976. Coal widows are as common as lunch pails in Eastern Kentucky. What happened to these fifteen widows had never before happened in the Kentucky coal fields. They became, through a remarkable twist of circumstance, the widows who sued the coal company—and won.

This is the story of those fifteen women, "The Scotia Widows," and their lawsuit against Big Daddy Coal.

# CONTENTS

# THE SCOTIA
# WIDOWS

# CHAPTER 1

# The Scotia Widows

Reda Turner of Cumberland, Kentucky, knew coal mining was dangerous. When she was fifteen years old her father died in a coal mine roof collapse. He left behind eleven children in the days before workers' compensation benefits provided some minimal aid for a dead miner's family. Reda remembered, "It was hard on Mom. I can remember lots of times when we barely had enough to eat, just gravy for supper and breakfast lots of days." Tragedy struck again four years later, when Reda's older brother was electrocuted in the Scotia mine.

When Reda married Dean Turner, her childhood sweetheart, her "fairy tale love," they left Eastern Kentucky for Detroit, where he found work. They had been living there a few years when they took a family trip back home. While there, Dean decided to apply for work at Scotia so they could stay in Kentucky and he could earn more than he was making in Detroit. Reda "tried to get Dean not to go in the mines, but he said they were paying twenty-six dollars a day and that would be good for our security. He wanted the best for his family." On March 9, 1976, they had been back in Kentucky for six years.

That morning, after Dean left for work at Scotia, Reda took their children to school and went to her aunt's house. While she was there, someone called to ask if everything was all right, because they had heard ambulances go by. Reda said everything was fine and went on to the store to buy ham for Dean's lunch bucket for the next day. She heard the checkout boy say "something about Scotia, but it didn't dawn on me what he said." She picked up her lunch items, and when she went to check out she asked him, "Did I hear you say something about Scotia?" He replied, "Yes, they had an explosion up there, and they have some men trapped." Reda "just went to pieces then." Her husband, Willie Dean Turner, was thirty-two years old. They had two children.

Vickie Scott heard a man over a CB radio at a friend's house frantically calling out, "We need help over at Scotia." She told him to "slow down, take it easy and tell me real slow what happened." When he excitedly repeated that there was an explosion at Scotia, she hesitantly asked, "What mine was it?" He said it was in a lower mine, so with great trepidation she asked if he knew what section the explosion happened in. He said it was in the Two Southeast Mains section. Vickie "knew that was where my husband was working. I just fell apart right there." Tommy Scott was twenty-four years old. They had no children.

Carol Combs was cleaning her home about ten miles from the mine when she heard an ambulance go up the road. She gave it no thought until a few minutes later when she was sweeping her porch. A neighbor rushed over to tell her there had been a serious accident at the mine, and she thought Carol should go there. Carol's husband, Everett Combs, was twenty-eight years old. They had two children.

Some of the miners' wives were urged to stay at home with loved ones until someone could obtain information about what had occurred at the mine. Diana McKnight waited to hear news of her husband, Larry, and of her brother, Everett Combs, both of whom were still in the mine. Larry was twenty-seven years old. He and Diana had one child.

But Geraldine McKnight did not stay home. She rushed to the mine after her mother called from the hospital to say they were emptying hospital beds for new arrivals because something had happened at Scotia. Geraldine's husband, Roy McKnight, a six-foot eight-inch bull-shouldered giant of a man, was known as Big Sack. He was thirty years old, and he and Geraldine had two children. She had faith that Big Sack, a former Army sergeant, would lead the men out alive.

At the mine, Geraldine McKnight and other anxious wives and their families had to walk a mile or so through mud, past ambulances and company vehicles, because the coal company would not let them park their cars on Scotia's property. They had to wait at the coal company bathhouse, where the miners each day would hoist their regular clothes to the ceiling and change into their mining clothes, steel-toed boots, hard hats, and the heavy leather belts which held their headlamp batteries and small metal emergency breathing devices called self-rescuers. At the end of their shift, the miners would shower off the black coal dust and grime from the mine and change back into their everyday clothes. That day, those regular clothes of the fifteen miners still somewhere underground were hanging above the women in the bathhouse. The wives and families of those fifteen men were told only that there had been an explosion.

The women suffered interminably as time ticked away without any information about their husbands. Scotia did not have a trained mine rescue team, so they had to wait for rescue teams from other companies to arrive. When these teams reached Scotia, they were briefed on what had occurred and then quickly went into the mine on rail cars as far as they could. There they set up a fresh air base and then worked their way on foot, as fast as possible, farther and farther into the mine. Time was their enemy, because the miners trapped somewhere underground were being exposed to the deadly carbon monoxide that follows a coal mine explosion, and their self-rescuers could provide breathable air for only a few hours. As the afternoon turned into the evening with no news from the rescue teams underground, the women at the surface grew ever more fearful that their husbands might not be found before their self-rescuers gave out.

Finally, at ten o'clock that night, a rescue team discovered the body of a dead miner. Word then came to the surface of three more bodies, and later three more were discovered. Some time after that, another rescue team reported that they had located six miners all together behind a partially constructed plastic barricade. At one-twenty the next morning, the bodies of the last two men were located.

About two in the morning, fourteen hours after the explosion, a minister stood on some boxes near the Scotia bathhouse and announced they had found all the men, which temporarily lifted the women's hopes. Then he added, "I'm sorry to inform you, there are no survivors." As he read the names of the fifteen men whose bodies had been found, the women shrieked in horror. Some fainted into the arms of their families. Carol Combs collapsed from shock and had to be taken away in an ambulance. She spent the next several days heavily sedated.

The wives of the fifteen miners were now widows. Unfortunately, they would not be the only women to lose their husbands that week to the Scotia mine. As soon as MESA, the Mining Enforcement Safety Administration, arrived, they took control of the Scotia mine. MESA asked for volunteers to accompany some MESA inspectors back into the mine to restore the ventilation, so the government could begin to establish the cause of the Scotia explosion. Then, two days after the March 9 explosion, while three MESA inspectors and ten volunteer miners were down in the mine working on the ventilation, the Scotia mine exploded again, killing the MESA inspectors and eight of the volunteers. Two volunteers working farther away from the blast and closer to the mine entrance escaped without injury. When other rescue teams reached the bodies of the eleven men, twenty-four hours after this second explosion, they found no signs of life. Because of the possibility of a third explosion, these rescue teams were ordered to return to the surface without recovering the eleven bodies. MESA then ordered the Scotia mine sealed.

# CHAPTER 2

# Déjà Vu

This infamous and deadly Scotia coal mine disaster inspired Congress to speedily enact the landmark Federal Mine Safety and Health Act of 1977. But recent coal mine explosions in Utah and West Virginia prove we have learned very little since Scotia. Coal production and profits still trump safety, and MESA—now called the Mine Safety and Health Administration—still responds more quickly to the coal operators and their lobbyists than it does to the safety needs of coal miners.

In August 2007, more than thirty years after the Scotia mine exploded, the Crandall Canyon coal mine in Utah collapsed, trapping six coal miners underground more than three miles from the mine entrance. Once again a coal mine disaster riveted us to our television sets, with its sadly familiar images of grieving wives, children, and parents, and black-faced miners nervously waiting for word on their friends below. Once again we prayed that the rapidly gathered rescue teams of volunteer coal miners could reach the endangered men in time. Some of us also recognized that our anxiety over the fate of these men was connected to our own primordial fear of being buried alive.

We were transfixed, our daily lives put on hold as they have been after major disasters at the World Trade Center in New York, or the Federal Building in Oklahoma City, or in earlier, similar Appalachian coal mine explosions such as those at Scotia. When there is an underground explosion or fire, coal miners are trained to put on their self-rescuers and to try to escape immediately to the surface. With the self-rescuer, a miner can survive for only a short time, depending on the amount of carbon monoxide in the air, so when the explosion blocks their escape route, they are told to build a quick barricade in a corner of the mine to keep the smoke and toxic gases from reaching them. They also are supposed to bang on something metal so their exact location can be pinpointed by seismic machines on the surface, and then to await rescue.

At Crandall Canyon, the families' vigil for the trapped miners lasted eleven paralyzing days as mine rescue teams tried to dig their way through the rubble in the mine to reach the place where the men might have barricaded themselves. During those eleven days, weary miners at the surface also drilled eight different bore holes deep into the mine to bring fresh air, food, and water to the men, if they could ever pinpoint exactly where they were. They even put a robotic camera down one of the bore holes. Despite their extraordinary efforts, they could detect no sight or sound of the men.

Meanwhile, volunteer rescue teams had worked their way down into the Crandall Canyon mine, burrowing feverishly for days and days through the wreckage of the mine passageways. On the eleventh day of their herculean labors, when they were still less than halfway to where the six miners had last been working, the mine collapsed on the rescuers, killing three of them, an eerie replay of what had happened at Scotia many years earlier. After that, further rescue attempts were suspended, the mine was sealed, and the six miners were never found.

About a year before these two recent Crandall Canyon mine collapses, a coal mine explosion in Sago, West Virginia, confined thirteen coal miners two miles underground. Before the rescue teams could enter the mine to search for them, the mine had to be cleared of dangerously high levels of carbon monoxide from the blast. That took almost twelve hours, but finally the rescue teams were permitted to begin excavating through the mine's ruins. Forty-one hours after that mine exploded they found the men.

Miraculously, one young man, twenty-seven-year-old Randal McCloy, Jr., was still alive, though only barely. They brought him out on a stretcher in a coma, and after he was hospitalized and underwent months of rehabilitation, he recovered to testify to the horror the men had faced. He said they had to share their self-rescuers because four of them did not work. The smoke and gases made it impossible for them to find an escape route, so they hung a plastic curtain back in the mine where they had been working, to try to make a leakproof barricade. They hammered for hours on bolts and steel plates to signal their location, but they heard no response from the surface. Two men left the barricade and tried a second time to find a way out, but they quickly returned, coughing and gagging. The battery-powered headlamps on the miners' hard hats eventually went out, leaving them in total darkness. Mr. McCloy said he lay as low as possible behind the barricade and took shallow breaths. Eventually the carbon monoxide seeped in behind their barricade, and their self-rescuers no longer were able to provide any more breathable air.

One by one they drifted off, poisoned by the carbon monoxide from the explosion, leaving only a moaning Randal McCloy, Jr. That is why the rescue teams never give up until they have reached the men underground. Even after forty-one hours, they may still save the life of one of their friends or fellow miners.

# CHAPTER 3

# "Blew All Our Minds"

The Appalachian coal fields in Eastern Kentucky, Eastern Tennessee, Virginia, and West Virginia have suffered from a long history of coal mine explosions, usually caused by the buildup of unventilated methane, a dangerous gas almost always found accompanying a coal seam. As the coal is mined, methane escapes into the mine and becomes combustible when it reaches levels between 5 and 15 percent of the surrounding air. Within those percentages, the slightest spark can ignite a methane explosion. Unfortunately, methane is also odorless, tasteless, and colorless, so it is hard to know when methane in the air reaches the dangerous range.

For centuries, miners brought canaries into the coal mines to alert them to methane accumulations. Canaries have a highly sensitive metabolism, so when they stopped chirping, fell off their perches, or died, overcome by methane, the miners quickly evacuated the mine. Eventually miners started using methane gas detectors to check methane levels before each shift, and deploying extensive ventilation machinery to keep fresh air flowing through all the portals of the mine. From its beginning the Scotia mine was known to be very "gassy," releasing above-normal levels of methane and requiring far-reaching ventilation procedures. Huge fans at the surface were required to suck air through all six sections of the Scotia mine to sweep out any methane released by the coal mining. However, despite numerous federal and state laws requiring ventilation of gassy coal mines, accidents still happen when laws are violated or proper safety precautions are ignored. That is what happened at Scotia.

Typically, after coal mine disasters the coal company quickly contacts the widows to offer them some token payment, and to ask them to sign a waiver against any litigation rights they might have against the coal company. So the Scotia Coal Company authorized its adjusters to offer the families of the fifteen miners the amounts required under Kentucky's workers' compensation laws, plus an additional five thousand dollars if the women would sign a release of any and all possible claims against Scotia. To warn the Scotia women not to sign anything, Sally Maggard and Barbara Callahan of the Council of Southern Mountains, a volunteer group founded by Kentucky missionaries, took to their cars to track down the fifteen widows, who were still living at home or with kinfolk. Fortunately, Sally and Barbara beat the coal company to almost all the women. Only one signed a release, which was immediately voided.

The history of workers' compensation laws explains why the payments required under those statutes are so minimal. During the early days of industrialization in our country, when employees sued to recover for their on-the-job damages, they were thrown out of court by an "unholy trinity" of court-created employer defenses. Judges protecting employers ruled that employees "assumed the risk" when they took the job, or that the employees' own "contributory negligence" helped cause their injury, or that a "fellow employee" caused their injury. For these reasons employees, and their widows, were denied any right to recover compensation for work-related injuries or deaths. To make some amends, and after great pressure from unions and other reformers, starting in the early 1900s, states enacted workers' compensation laws to require employers to provide some modest relief for job-related accidents without requiring the employees to prove who was at fault. However, in return for these guaranteed, though small, workers' compensation recoveries, employees and their families had to relinquish their right to bring any lawsuit against the employer to recover any greater damage payments. Thus, in Kentucky, the Scotia Coal Company was required to pay some workers' compensation payments to the families of the coal miners who died while on the job, only about $192 every two weeks, subject to a cap on the total amount to be paid, and also subject to termination of any further compensation, except a two-year lump-sum payment, if the miner's widow remarried. In exchange, the families of the deceased coal miners were prohibited from suing Scotia for any greater recovery.

Soon after the Scotia mine explosion, Dan Hendrickson of the Council of Southern Mountains called me to ask if I could represent the Scotia widows. I was a lawyer in Washington, D.C., and Dan knew I had recently finished a successful two-year-long litigation against the Pittston Company to prove its responsibility for the Buffalo Creek coal mining disaster in West Virginia. In that case, a recklessly built coal waste dam collapsed, unleashing more than one hundred thirty million gallons of black coal wastewater and sludge on sixteen small communities. This twenty-to-thirty-foot tidal wave of rampaging black water killed one hundred twenty-five people, mostly women and children, and left thousands homeless. At that time I was the public interest partner at Arnold and Porter, a prestigious Washington, D.C., law firm, and the partners of the firm agreed that I could represent 625 of the survivors. The lawsuit we brought established that survivors are entitled to compensation not only for the loss of the earning power of their loved ones and their homes and possessions, but also for their own mental suffering, what is now officially called "post-traumatic stress disorder." I wrote a book about that case, *The Buffalo Creek Disaster,* which was published in 1976, soon after the Scotia mine explosion.

I told Dan I was reluctant to engage in another protracted coal company fight. It would take years and cost a substantial amount of money, and I also did not see how the Scotia widows could avoid Kentucky's workers' compensation laws, which immunized the Scotia Coal Company from a lawsuit. So I begged off and said I could not represent them.

Two months after the Scotia explosion, a joint congressional labor subcommittee held hearings in Kentucky and then later in Washington, D.C., into the causes of the explosion. The women who attended these hearings were shocked to learn how unsafe the Scotia mine was. They knew coal mining was dangerous, but they had also assumed Scotia's managers were taking every required precaution to make the mine as safe as possible for their husbands. Before the explosion, when coal prices were high and the pay was good, some of the women had returned with their husbands to Eastern Kentucky, where the men could earn a good living mining coal. Denver Widner, his wife, Charlotte, and their two children had returned only two years earlier, after Denver had spent three years in the Army and eight years at General Motors. At Scotia, the men were earning from fifteen thousand to twenty-five thousand dollars a year. But until these hearings, the wives had not really understood the danger their husbands faced to make those paychecks.

As the congressional report noted, Scotia "apparently found it cheaper to pay the fines for its numerous safety violations of federal ventilation standards [thirty-three times in the fifteen months prior to the explosion] than to comply with the law." The highest penalty assessed against Scotia in the fourteen months prior to the explosion was $585, later reduced to $291. The only safety inspector employed by Scotia testified he did not conduct a single fire or evacuation drill in the three and a half years prior to the explosion. The miners were rarely trained in the use of the self-rescuer breathing devices they carried with them. The report concluded, "It was a mine which . . . placed production and profit before the health and safety of its miners."

Six of the miners did not die immediately at the time of the Scotia explosion. According to the rescue teams which found them, these six men apparently tried to escape only to find that the smoke and gases and debris from the explosion seemed to block their route to the surface more than three miles away. So they put on their self-rescuers and erected a temporary plastic curtain where they had been mining. There they waited for rescue, in vain, behind their hastily built barricade. At the hearing, their wives heard a safety expert testify that these six miners, using their self-rescuers, could probably have walked safely out of the mine. But these men had not been properly trained in self-rescuer use or evacuation procedures.

After the hearings and the congressional report, some of the women determined to seek vengeance of some kind against Scotia and the bosses who operated the mine. Their grief had turned to rage. Jennifer Boggs had lost her husband, Dennis, in the Scotia mine explosion. Dennis was twenty-six years old. He and Jennie had one child. What she learned at those hearings "blew all our minds." Jennie now wanted somehow to inflict pain on Scotia. "I want to see Scotia pay for this. It's just not right to let them off Scot free. . . ."

By this time, Dan Hendrickson had given Jennie a copy of my book, *The Buffalo Creek Disaster*, and told the women about my lawsuit for the Buffalo Creek survivors. He understood why I thought the workers' compensation laws precluded the women from suing Scotia, but he could not convince the women there was nothing they could do. He thought maybe they would trust me if I flew to Kentucky and explained to them why they could not bring a successful lawsuit, so I agreed. I said I would tell the women I thought the best they could do was to accept their workers' compensation checks and try to move on with their lives.

# CHAPTER 4

# Big Daddy Coal

I met with most of the fifteen widows in a community college classroom in Cumberland, Kentucky. They were furious with Scotia, the "Big Daddy" coal company that was supposed to have been taking good care of the coal miners and their families. They were also angry with their own dads and brothers and brothers-in-law, many of whom still worked for Scotia, because some of these men kept telling them not to make trouble for Scotia. These young Appalachian women were used to listening to the strong men around them tell them what was best for them. But not anymore.

I did my best to explain to the women why Kentucky law prohibited them from suing the Scotia Coal Company, and after they had vented their feelings it seemed they finally recognized the futility of litigation. As I was leaving, Libby Gibbs hesitantly asked whether she should go ahead now and cash the workers' compensation checks she had been receiving. Libby's husband, David, had been twenty-nine years old. His death had left her with two children to support, but she and some of the other women had not cashed their workers' compensation checks, not wanting to give up any rights they might have against Scotia. I looked at Libby's checks and noticed there were four boxes at the top of each check—one for Scotia Coal Company, one for Stearns Coal Company, one for Blue Diamond Mining, Inc., and one for Harris Mining Company. There was an X mark in the Scotia Coal Company box on each of her workers' compensation checks, identifying her husband as an employee of the Scotia Coal Company.

When I asked about the companies listed on the checks, the women explained that Scotia and the three other mining companies were owned by the Blue Diamond Coal Company of Knoxville, Tennessee. I was confused. I had never heard about the Blue Diamond Coal Company. I had one of those lightbulb moments when the mind tells you to be alert to something, and you *really* listen. I told Libby and the other women they could cash their workers' compensation checks without waiving any rights and said I was going back to my office in Washington to see if I could find a way around Scotia's workers' compensation immunity. Maybe the women could sue the Scotia Coal Company's sole share-holder, the Blue Diamond Coal Company.

Normally, you cannot sue a shareholder of a corpora-tion for any wrongdoing the corporation engages in, be-cause there is a "corporate veil" between a corporation and its shareholders, and a plaintiff cannot "pierce the corporate veil" to sue the shareholders. This allows peo-ple all over the United States, and indeed the world, to buy shares in corporations without fear of being sued if the corporation runs afoul of the law. Of course, you can sue the corporation directly for its own wrong-doing.

I understood the prohibition against suing the sole shareholder of a corporation even when that sole share-holder is itself a corporation. That was the Pittston Company's defense when we sued it in the Buffalo Creek case. In that case Pittston, the parent corporation, was the sole stockholder of its subsidiary corporation, the Buffalo Mining Company. Pittston argued that because it was a separate company from its wholly owned sub-sidiary, I could not pierce the corporate veil of the Buf-falo Mining Company and sue Pittston. We responded that Pittston and the Buffalo Mining Company were really one company, like one ball of wax, that Pittston had not run its subsidiary corporation as a separate company, that there were no real shareholder meetings of the Buffalo Mining Company, and that Pittston even called the Buffalo Mining Company a "division," rather than a subsidiary, of Pittston. At the outset of that case, we had just enough evidence that the two companies really were only one company to persuade the judge to let us pursue our case against Pittston.

Maybe now I could argue just the opposite. If I could prove that the Blue Diamond Coal Company scrupulously ran the Scotia Coal Company as a separate company, maybe Blue Diamond would not be allowed to pierce its own subsidiary's corporate veil and wrap itself in Scotia's immunity. If I could win that argument, the widows could sue Blue Diamond, not as the sole stockholder of the Scotia Coal Company, but directly for Blue Diamond's own independent negligence, if any, in causing the Scotia mine explosion. Of course, I had no evidence to prove that Blue Diamond, when looked at separately and apart from Scotia and Scotia's employees, was responsible for the Scotia explosion. But that was a different problem. The first obstacle was whether the parent-shareholder could be sued at all.

I went to a law library in Washington, D.C., to read

workers' compensation treatises and to look up state law cases on corporate immunity. For many hours I pulled books from the shelves, trying to find at least one judicial opinion where a judge had allowed a parent corporation to be sued for the death of an employee of one of its subsidiaries. Law books from states all over the country piled up on the table around me as I chased down opinion after opinion. I found a few helpful state court cases, though none from Kentucky.

Finally I found a recent federal court case, the only relevant federal court opinion in the entire country, in which a federal judge had held that the estate of a deceased employee could sue a parent corporation for that parent company's negligence in causing the death of its subsidiary's employee. The parent claimed that it and its subsidiary corporation were one company, mere "alter egos" of each other; that the subsidiary corporation was "so managed and controlled by the parent that it was not an independent self-sustaining enterprise"; and that the two companies were the common employer of the deceased employee. So the parent company argued that under Tennessee's workers' compensation law it was entitled to share in its subsidiary corporation's immunity from suit.

Judge Robert L. Taylor, the federal judge in Knoxville, Tennessee, disagreed and ruled that the estate of the employee of the subsidiary corporation could maintain a common-law wrongful death action against the parent corporation despite the subsidiary corporation's immunity under Tennessee's workers' compensation statute. I read this case over and over to be sure it said what I thought it said. I had never spent a more exciting day in a library reading law cases. Now I had to decide what to do with what I had found.

Could my new law firm afford to represent the women, and, if so, did I want to be drawn again into a long, quixotic struggle against a powerful coal company? After the Buffalo Creek case was settled, I had left the comfort of the big Washington law firm where I had been a partner and started a small "boutique" law firm with two friends, Mitch Rogovin and Harry Huge. Rogovin, Stern and Huge was just the three of us and two associates, with only a few clients and large start-up expenses piling up for our new offices, furnishings, rent, typewriters, insurance, and salaries for our associates and secretaries. This lawsuit would be very costly for us, since we would have to pay all the expenses, and the women would have to reimburse us only if they won. We would also be spending countless hours of my time and the time of others in our firm, with no payment of any legal fees for that time unless the women succeeded with their lawsuit. Then, if they won, we would be entitled to a contingency fee of 25 percent of their recoveries, although there was no guarantee that 25 percent would be enough to equal the hourly fees we usually charged for our time.

After lengthy discussions with my partners about the difficulties and costs of filing and pursuing a lawsuit against Blue Diamond, they said they would back me if I wanted to represent the women. Now it was up to me.

I have an aversion to getting into something new, a fear that I will be entering quicksand, sucked in and unable to extricate myself. I cannot even talk with the person next to me on an airplane flight, afraid they will pull me into a lengthy, boring conversation while I am trapped in my seat with no escape. There are those who dip their toe in the water before going in the pool, and there are those who dive right in. I am a toe-dipper. On the other hand, once I enter something new, after slowly overcoming my reluctance, I then find I dig in so deeply and become so obsessed that I cut off those around me. That happened during the Buffalo Creek case, when I was not only physically absent in West Virginia for weeks at a time, but also mentally absent even when I was back home, my mind still constantly thinking about the problems and issues of the case. My wife and two-year-old son had suffered from my dual absences. I was fearful the same thing would happen again if I accepted the Scotia case. On the other hand, it was hard to turn my back on these widows, now that I had met them in person and seen their courageous determination to sue Big Daddy Coal. I discussed all this with my wife, and she too left the determination to me.

I wanted to take on the widows' case, in part because I was already in, having found a legal precedent that gave them some hope, but also because I wanted to prove that our victory in the Buffalo Creek lawsuit had not been a fluke. In that case, we had fortunately been assigned a federal judge willing to move our case along, and flexible enough to help us establish new legal precedent for the right of survivors to sue for mental suffering. I knew how unusual that experience was, because judges hostile to new ideas readily torpedo litigation they do not like. I had seen that happen during the civil rights days of the 1960s, when lawyers from the Civil Rights Division of the Justice Department, where I then was working, had to appear before racist Southern judges unwilling to forge new remedies for discrimination against black people trying to register to vote. But Judge Taylor appeared to be the kind of judge willing to respond to our unusual lawsuit. With his help, maybe we could pull off another surprising victory.

I flew back to Kentucky to meet with the women and tell them I would represent them if they wanted to sue the Blue Diamond Coal Company. I explained that they could rely on Judge Taylor's decision, although I cautioned them that his decision was based on Tennessee's workers' compensation statute, while their case would be governed by Kentucky's workers' compensation laws. I told them I even thought they could sue Blue Diamond in Judge Taylor's court in Tennessee, since Blue Diamond was headquartered in Knoxville. Of course, it was a long shot, since they would first have to establish that Blue Diamond was not immune from suit under Kentucky law in order to stay in court, and then they would have to prove that Blue Diamond itself did something that caused the explosion. I made it very clear that the odds were greatly against them. But they were angry and ready to try anything, despite the odds. So was I. Together we decided to roll the dice.

# CHAPTER 5

# On the Road

I was on the road again, driving through shadowed hollows and valleys, surrounded by the dark, hovering, steep mountains of Eastern Kentucky coal country, past log cabins and run-down shacks, with smoke curling up from chimneys in the evening as night fell on the Cumberland Mountains. The Eastern Kentucky lawyer Harry Caudill wrote a beautiful book, *Night Comes to the Cumberlands,* about the foggy mist which rises each morning and descends each night on these old Appalachian Mountains, home to such hard-working, but mostly poverty-ridden, people. I was happy, smiling as I drove around, my radio tuned to a local country music station, window down, elbow resting on the sill, calling on each woman individually, ready to slay a dragon.

They welcomed me and fed me well. I felt privileged to be invited into their lives, to sit around their kitchen tables and visit with them. Sometimes their fathers and brothers were present and forcefully argued against a lawsuit, so I would try to persuade them that their daughters and sisters had a chance to obtain much more for their families than the basic workers' compensation payments, but I usually failed to change anyone's mind. Finally, the women would have the men leave, and we would discuss their lawsuit. I questioned them at length to obtain any facts they had about the Scotia mine and about the Blue Diamond Coal Company, and looked through any payroll records or other papers they and their husbands had received. I compiled a detailed history of their deceased husbands, confirmed their marriages, took them through the filing of the papers necessary for each of them to be named the executor of her husband's estate, and had each sign a retainer letter with our law firm.

Two of the women, Vera Galloway and Celinda Sparkman, had already retained Eugene Goss, a lawyer in Harlan, Kentucky. Vera and her husband, Earl, who had been forty-three, had one child. Celinda and her husband, Ivan, who had been thirty-three, had two children. Another woman, Ethel Sturgill, had hired a lawyer in Whitesburg, Kentucky. Her husband, Jimmy, had been twenty years old, and Ethel was pregnant with their first child. I met with these plaintiffs' lawyers to see if they would allow me to take the lead in a lawsuit for all the women.

Gene Goss welcomed me into his second floor walk-up law office on Main Street, directly across from the Harlan County courthouse. He said he had checked up on me in Martindale-Hubbell, a lawyer referral book, and discovered that I had an AV rating. So he was willing to throw his two cases in with mine, particularly after I explained that I thought I could find a way around Scotia's immunity by suing Blue Diamond in Tennessee. The local lawyer representing Ethel Sturgill also agreed to have me take the lead in his case.

When I returned to Washington, I looked in Martindale to learn that an AV peer review rating means that "a lawyer has reached the height of professional excellence. He or she has usually practiced law for many years, and is recognized for the highest levels of skill and integrity." Wow! I was impressed. I didn't know I had such a rating. But was that really me? I had just turned thirty-seven and did not look like someone who had "practiced law for many years" to reach "the height of professional excellence." In fact, I thought I appeared too young, so I had grown a full, dark, bushy beard to make me seem more mature. My wife said I looked like a mountain man. That was good enough, so I kept the beard, even though others thought I looked like a hippie.

I flew back to Knoxville to meet J. D. Lee, the lawyer who had won the federal case before Judge Taylor that we now would rely on. J. D. Lee, one of Tennessee's best plaintiff's lawyers, was nationally known as a past president of the Association of Trial Lawyers of America. I told him what we planned to do, and he agreed to be our local counsel in Knoxville.

I began to draft the complaint. We wanted to bring our case in Judge Taylor's federal court for the Eastern District of Tennessee because of his favorable opinion, a ruling upheld by the United States Court of Appeals for the Sixth Circuit, and because we had to stay out of Eastern Kentucky, where the coal companies had greater economic and political power than they had in Knoxville, Tennessee. So our first hurdle was to craft a lawsuit which could be filed in a Tennessee federal court.

Federal courts are open to citizens of different states if there is "complete diversity of citizenship," meaning all of the plaintiffs have to reside in a different state from the defendant. The fifteen women who would be the named plaintiffs, as representatives of their deceased husbands' estates, lived in Kentucky and Virginia. The defendant, Blue Diamond, was incorporated in Delaware, so it was considered a Delaware citizen. It looked as though we had the required complete diversity of citizenship to sue in a Tennessee federal court.

But a corporation is also deemed a citizen of the state of its principal place of business. So we alleged that Blue Diamond's principal place of business was at its headquarters in Tennessee. Again, we had complete diversity between the Kentucky and Virginia women as plaintiffs suing a Delaware corporation having its principal place of business in Tennessee. We had cleared our first hurdle and could file our lawsuit in Judge Taylor's federal court in Knoxville, Tennessee.

We now turned our attention to the second important hurdle: proof that Blue Diamond caused the explosion. We did not have any expert report on the actual cause of the explosion, so we merely alleged that Blue Diamond knew, or should have known, that there was inadequate ventilation in the Two Southeast Mains section of the Scotia mine where the explosion occurred. We asked for thirty million dollars in compensatory damages—for the loss of the earning power of the decedents, for the pain and suffering of the men before they died, and for the pain and suffering of the widows. And we asked for an additional thirty million dollars in punitive damages for Blue Diamond's recklessness in allowing Scotia to continue to mine coal from an unsafe, improperly ventilated, gassy coal mine emitting over half a million cubic feet of methane a day, the most of any coal mine in Eastern Kentucky at that time.

With these two hurdles cleared and mounting confidence in our case, I flew back to Knoxville and accompanied J. D. Lee as he filed our complaint with the clerk in the federal courthouse in Knoxville. J.D. demonstrated why he was such an effective lawyer. When we entered the courthouse building, he did not go directly to the clerk's office. Instead, he stopped in the marshal's office and talked with his friends there, telling them about the case he was about to file for fifteen widows, and their twenty-four children left without fathers, after the explosion at Blue Diamond's coal mine in Eastern Kentucky. He talked about Blue Diamond's willingness to let an unsafe mine continue to operate so it could produce more coal to sell, without taking care to protect the men who had to toil deep down in that gassy mine every day for their bosses back in Knoxville.

When we left the marshal's office, he talked with each person we passed in the hallways on our way to the clerk's office. Once there, he explained our case again to the clerks. By the time we actually filed the complaint, everyone in the courthouse was rooting for us. The clerk's office assigned our case to Judge Taylor, since he was the only federal judge sitting in Knoxville.

Blue Diamond hired Bert Combs, a living legend in Eastern Kentucky, to represent them. He was born in Eastern Kentucky and went on to graduate second in his class from the University of Kentucky law school. During World War II he was a captain on the legal staff of General Douglas MacArthur in the Pacific and helped prepare evidence against Japanese war criminals. After a short stint in the Kentucky state attorney general's office, he served for four years as a judge on Kentucky's highest court. He then ran for and was elected governor of Kentucky, the first Kentucky governor to come from Eastern Kentucky. He was a very popular governor, probably one of the best governors in Kentucky history. President Lyndon Johnson later appointed him to serve as a federal judge on the United States Sixth Circuit Court of Appeals, the court with appellate jurisdiction over all the federal judges and federal cases from Kentucky and Tennessee. He presided as a judge on the Sixth Circuit in Cincinnati for four years before returning to Louisville to practice law.

By the time of the Scotia case, Bert Combs was a white-haired, kindly-looking gentleman, with what folks called a "way-down-yonder drawl." It was his job to obtain a dismissal of our case, or at least to have it transferred out of Tennessee and back to Eastern Kentucky so he could fight us on his home turf.

So Blue Diamond immediately filed a motion to dismiss our case from federal court, asserting that Blue Diamond was a citizen of Kentucky because its principal place of business was Kentucky, where its subsidiary corporations owned many mines. Therefore, they alleged, there was no diversity of citizenship between Blue Diamond of Kentucky and the thirteen plaintiffs who lived in Kentucky. We responded that the "nerve center" of Blue Diamond's operations was Knoxville, Tennessee, where it had its headquarters, seventy-three employees, and all its executive offices, engineers, accountants, and sales personnel; that Blue Diamond had significant business outside Kentucky, in Tennessee, North Carolina, and Virginia; and that most of Blue Diamond's income came from selling coal, which also occurred outside Kentucky. Our chance to stay in federal court hung in the balance. Was Blue Diamond's principal place of business in Kentucky, where it mined its coal and where the Scotia explosion occurred? Or was Blue Diamond's principal place of business in Tennessee, where it controlled its mining subsidiaries from its Knoxville headquarters?

Judges are people who often let their emotions come into play. They are not automatons, hearing the facts, reading the laws and relevant court precedents, and then dispensing judgment without feeling. The precedents are not always clear, and when there is doubt, or where the law actually leaves the decision explicitly to the judgment of the judge, judge they do. You often win when a judge is sympathetic to the facts of your case. And when their sympathies lie with the other side, you usually lose.

Blue Diamond's counsel started off on the wrong foot. Judge Taylor felt they were playing fast and loose with him by arguing that Blue Diamond had its principal place of business in Kentucky, when Blue Diamond's counsel had assured him in an earlier case that Blue Diamond's principal place of business was Tennessee. In that prior case, Judge Taylor noted, Blue Diamond's "reputable counsel" had signed a complaint alleging that "Blue Diamond is a corporation with its principal place of business at Knoxville, Tennessee." Judge Taylor was not going to let Blue Diamond's counsel reverse the position they had asked him to adopt earlier:

> Blue Diamond used this forum less than ten years ago, to try a very difficult case, when a Kentucky court might have been a more appropriate forum. Blue Diamond now seeks to convince the Court that it should be treated as a "stranger" in Tennessee, and . . . not be considered a Tennessee resident when sued by an outsider. Blue Diamond is no stranger to citizens of this state, or to this Court.

He dismissed Blue Diamond's motion, finding that its principal place of business was at its headquarters in Tennessee. We had complete diversity of citizenship and could stay in federal court. Now the question was, which federal court?

Blue Diamond had also filed a motion to transfer the trial of our case, for the convenience of the parties, to a federal judge in Eastern Kentucky, if Blue Diamond's motion to dismiss for lack of diversity was denied. We desperately wanted to avoid Eastern Kentucky, not only because Blue Diamond was the big employer there, but also because Bert Combs, the Eastern Kentucky hero, would have such great sway with an Eastern Kentucky judge and jury. Indeed, the eighty-mile-long highway that Bert Combs had championed while he was governor, to connect Eastern Kentucky to the rest of the state, had just been named the Bert T. Combs Mountain Parkway in his honor.

Blue Diamond had a good argument this time. A federal court trial in Eastern Kentucky would be more convenient for the fifteen women and the witnesses, since most of them resided in Eastern Kentucky. And it would be more appropriate to have a Kentucky federal judge, rather than a Tennessee federal judge, interpret Kentucky workers' compensation law. On the other hand, we argued that the docket of pending criminal and civil cases in the Eastern District of Kentucky was so crowded we would never obtain a trial in a reasonable time. The women could expect a speedier trial in Tennessee, where there was a less crowded docket.

I thought we could persuade Judge Taylor to keep our case, but unexpectedly he was assigned to Baltimore to preside over the criminal trial of Governor Marvin Mandel of Maryland for mail fraud and racketeering, our nation's first criminal trial of a sitting governor. We were devastated by this unfortunate twist of fate. Judge Taylor reluctantly had to agree that he might have to transfer our case to Eastern Kentucky, but insisted he would do so only if we could be guaranteed a trial "within a reasonable time."

# CHAPTER 6

# "That Dog Won't Hunt"

**B**ert Combs immediately undertook to obtain a trial of our case in Eastern Kentucky "within a reasonable time." Judge H. David Hermansdorfer was the federal district judge in the Eastern District of Kentucky at Pikeville, the federal courthouse nearest to the Scotia mine. He was a graduate of Princeton, spent three years in Army intelligence, graduated from the University of Virginia law school, became a successful corporate lawyer in Eastern Kentucky representing energy interests, flew his own airplane, was a member of many corporate boards, and was a prominent conservative Republican. He had been nominated to the federal district court by President Nixon only a few years before the Scotia mine disaster. For his Senate confirmation he agreed to resign from a "substantial number" of his corporate positions to avoid any conflict of interest. We will see how serious he would be about avoiding conflicts of interest.

Judge Hermansdorfer, a severe-looking man with dark-rimmed glasses, was well known to Bert Combs, who had appeared before him in an earlier coal mine disaster case. In that case, Combs had persuaded Judge Hermansdorfer to dismiss the most significant count of a criminal indictment against a coal company and one of its owners for violating federal safety standards, which had allegedly caused a coal mine explosion near Hyden, Kentucky, killing thirty-eight men.

Now Bert Combs would try to have our case transferred to Judge Hermansdorfer, who had thoughts of being elevated to the United States Court of Appeals for the Sixth Circuit. As a Republican, Judge Hermansdorfer did not stand a good chance, since Jimmy Carter was the newly elected Democratic president. But Combs was a major Democratic leader in Kentucky, and he was close to President Carter, who had just appointed him to the President's General Advisory Committee on Arms Control and Disarmament. It probably would not be wise to be on the wrong side of Bert Combs, especially if you hoped a Democratic president might elevate you to the Sixth Circuit.

Judge Hermansdorfer had a very crowded criminal and civil docket, with criminal cases, and numerous other categories of cases, entitled by law to speedy trials before civil cases like ours. Nevertheless, Judge Hermansdorfer readily agreed to set an early trial date for our civil case, so Judge Taylor transferred it to him. Judge Hermansdorfer immediately set a trial date for our case seven months later in Pikeville, Kentucky, a year and a half after the explosion. Bert Combs and his team were ecstatic. They had the Scotia case where they wanted it, in Eastern Kentucky before Judge Hermansdorfer.

I went back on the road to visit the women to try to comfort them. We had been able to keep their case in federal court, but now we were in the wrong federal court, and our chances looked grim. The women faced other pressures as well. They were feeling ostracized by their families and friends for taking on Big Daddy Coal. Why were they making trouble for Scotia, which employed so many husbands, fathers, and sons of Eastern Kentucky? They were also being talked about, with people gossiping about their trying to recover sixty million dollars, an enormous sum in their part of the world. Some people complained, "What do they need with so much money?" Others heard rumors that the women had already received thousands of dollars because of their husbands' deaths. Libby Gibbs came home one night to find the rooms of her house ripped apart, the couch cut to pieces and turned over, drawers and papers and clothing strewn everywhere by someone looking for her supposed riches. They could not find what they wanted, so they took eggs and threw them all over the walls, and took a half gallon of ice cream from the freezer and left it on the television to melt. Libby had to take her two boys and move in with her in-laws.

They were being called, derogatorily, "the Scotia widows," out for even more money than the workers' compensation checks they were already receiving. They hated being called the Scotia widows because it made them sound as if they were Scotia's property. They were no one's property. They were freeing themselves from Big Daddy Coal, which controlled so much of Eastern Kentucky, from their own dads and brothers who worked in the mines, and even from many of their old friends.

The fact that the women would have a trial in seven months at least meant they had an end in sight. But Bert Combs, backed by Judge Hermansdorfer, would prove to be a formidable foe. Judge Hermansdorfer issued almost no decisions in our case prior to the trial, rulings we needed to help guide the trial, to determine which documents would be admissible, and to know what evidence the jury would be allowed to see. We also kept pushing for discovery about Blue Diamond's involvement in the affairs of the Scotia mine and did obtain one hearing on a discovery issue before Judge Hermansdorfer's magistrate. We wanted access to Blue Diamond's finances to help show its direct involvement in the operations of the Scotia mine and its financial ability to pay large punitive damages; but our argument fell on deaf ears. As the magistrate explained to us, in the legal language of Eastern Kentucky, "That dog won't hunt."

As we neared the trial date, we took sworn deposition testimony from Blue Diamond's executives. We rented a room, placed a long table in the middle with a court reporter at one end, and then sat ourselves across the table from the Blue Diamond witnesses. They were flanked by many lawyers, including Bert Combs, other partners and associates from his Louisville firm, and Blue Diamond's defense and insurance lawyers from Pikeville, Hazard, Lexington, Bluefield, and Knoxville. On our side of the table, I had the support of lawyers from my firm, and sometimes Gene Goss. During their depositions, Blue Diamond's executives constantly testified that Blue Diamond and Scotia were all one company. During the break at one of those depositions, I noticed a wadded-up piece of paper left in the ashtray. It read, "one ball of wax." That was their mantra. No one could separate what Blue Diamond's employees may have done or not done from what Scotia's employees did or did not do, so there was no way, Blue Diamond thought, that it alone could be blamed for the explosion.

Still I tried to prove that Blue Diamond and Scotia were separate by questioning Blue Diamond's officials about their long history of animosity against the United Mine Workers of America union. One of the major reasons Scotia was incorporated and operated separately from Blue Diamond was to ensure that even if the coal miners' union succeeded in unionizing the employees at one Blue Diamond mine, that unionization would not carry over to another separately incorporated Blue Diamond mine like the Scotia mine. Now we would hoist Blue Diamond on its own petard—legalese for saying Blue Diamond would now suffer the consequences of its own assiduous efforts to keep the Scotia Coal Company a separate, nonunion corporation.

Blue Diamond's lawyers also insisted on deposing each of the fifteen women, in part, I thought, to warn them they would face a difficult trial if they continued to pursue their case. Blue Diamond's counsel grilled the women over and over: Who paid for them to go to the congressional hearings in Washington? What was the involvement of the United Mine Workers? Who told them to hire me as their lawyer? Why were they uncomfortable with local Kentucky plaintiffs' lawyers? Were they obligated to pay the expenses of their lawsuit? Were they seeing other men? Had they remarried? The questions were mostly irrelevant, but in discovery, a lawyer is free to ask pretty wide-ranging questions.

Often George Frampton or Jonathan Schiller, lawyers from our law firm who had spent many days in Kentucky preparing the women for their depositions, would direct them not to answer these harassing questions. So Blue Diamond's lawyer would try to frighten the women, and their lawyers, by telling the court reporter at the deposition to type up the questions the witness refused to answer so he could quickly certify those questions for Judge Hermansdorfer to rule on. They never did take these improper questions to Judge Hermansdorfer, but it was intimidating nevertheless to hear the threat over and over as we continued to object to their efforts to bully the plaintiffs.

The women were also asked about the money and charitable donations they received after the explosion, as though they now were wealthy enough not to need any more money. Did you buy a new car? Do you have a new house? In fact, some of the women were struggling. Vickie Scott had to sell her CB equipment for sixty-five dollars, her car for fifteen hundred dollars, and her furniture for seventy-five dollars. She was working cleaning rooms at the Parkway Motel for a dollar fifty an hour. Scotia had also cut off their medical insurance after one year, so some of the women could no longer buy the medicine they needed for themselves and their children. Almost all of the women had suffered severe emotional problems since the explosion and had to take medication.

The children had suffered too. Reda Turner testified that her husband's truck was still parked in their driveway, "and one of my sons would just sit by the truck all the time and he would rub the sides of the truck." Some of the children were having nightmares and crying spells over their lost fathers. Ethel Sturgill's little son never did know his dad, Jimmy Sturgill, since Ethel was pregnant when he died in the mine. Similarly, Madonna Griffith was pregnant with their second child when her husband, Robert, died.

Reda Turner shared her grief and anger with us. She said she would send her children out of the house and cry for hours, throwing her husband's clothes around because she was angry with him for dying. She could not eat or sleep well for months and sometimes would go to the cemetery at night and throw the flowers off his grave, then replace them the next day. She said that around the anniversary of the explosion she tried to think of ways to ease her pain: "I try to stay busy so my mind is occupied, but it doesn't work." She and the other Scotia widows, and the children, were suffering from the post-traumatic stress disorder we had identified in our lawsuit for the survivors of the Buffalo Creek disaster.

Fortunately, the women had one another to provide some comfort. As Reda said, "Some of us became very close. We all knew there was somebody else going though the same thing. We could call each other in the middle of the night to talk and cry, and that made it easier. There's a bond that's very hard to explain." Jennifer Boggs agreed: "We have become closest friends now. We've been through so much together, both personally and through the lawsuit. And no one else really has been able to understand how we feel and what we've been up against."

No matter how much they hurt, the women were determined to see their lawsuit through to the end, wanting to show the world what Blue Diamond's recklessness had done to their husbands and children, and to their hopes and dreams. They also wanted to obtain enough money to provide for their children. As Jennifer Boggs said, "I would have given up at times, but my son Dennis needed to be raised! His dad would have provided for him if he hadn't been killed, and I intended to see that he got what he needed." During her deposition, we had Jennifer Boggs, alphabetically the lead plaintiff in our lawsuit entitled *Boggs v. Blue Diamond Coal Company*, identify a letter she had written soon after the explosion to Gordon Bonnyman, the largest shareholder, and the chairman of the board and president, of the Blue Diamond Coal Company:

I don't know exactly why I'm writing this but I do hope you'll take the time to read it. I don't know whose responsibility it was (and is) to see that Scotia is run properly but it wasn't (isn't) done. My husband loved to work there. He felt there was no danger and that he was indeed safe. Now he's six feet under the ground leaving behind a twenty four year old widow and a two year old son who love and miss him very much. He put his complete faith in you people. Someone let him and the other men down. Someone will pay!

I think that you should be taking some of the responsibility for this instead of putting it all on

Jasper Cornett [the Blue Diamond engineer in charge of mine ventilation]. My husband and the others worked their tails off so you and the other *big* men could have the luxuries of life. These men were young. Their lives were just beginning.

No one from Scotia has expressed their sympathy to me. No one said my husband was a good worker—we're going to miss him. I guess you think he was a machine too. When he broke down, all you'd have to do was replace him. I won't let you people forget those . . . men. I'll do every thing I can to make sure of that. I'm very bitter. My husband was my life. Now I have a two year old son to raise. A child that will never see how his daddy smiled or know the sound of his voice. Or most important—how much his daddy loved him. He was in that mine for us. And Scotia took him— Scotia and that almighty dollar.

We also marked Gordon Bonnyman's written response. He was a devout Catholic who had served with the United States Army in the Pacific theater during World War II, where he was awarded numerous medals including a Bronze Star with a cluster and a Chinese medal of merit. After the war he had come home to Knoxville to work in the family coal business started by his Scottish ancestors. Mr. Bonnyman wrote:

I have your letter. . . . I realize that the flowers sent to your husband's funeral were very inadequate to express my sympathy and regret. I do want you to know how you and the other survivors of the Scotia tragedies have been in the thoughts of everybody concerned with the operation.

The Scotia explosions had a greater effect emotionally on me than anything that has happened since my only brother was killed in the assault on Tarawa in World War II.

If there is anything that I can do personally to help you, please let me know and I will try to help. With deepest sympathy.

But flowers and sympathy were all Mr. Bonnyman and Blue Diamond offered. They made no effort to settle with the widows after their lawsuit was filed. At least one of them, Geraldine Coots, was not strong enough to stand up to Blue Diamond and to the pressures brought by her own family to withdraw from the lawsuit. She drove to her deposition in Pikeville, but then she refused to testify, turned around, and drove back home. Her husband, Virgil Coots, Jr., had been twenty-three years old. He and Geraldine had two children. We spent some time with Geraldine, trying to convince her of how important her lawsuit would be for her children, and for her, if we could win. But if she really did not want to pursue her suit, there was not much we could do. She finally agreed to try once more to appear at her deposition. This time she explained why she had turned back the first time:

> [M]y brother in law, and my mother and my other brother, Charlie, he worked for Scotia. . . . They had me shook up and I didn't know what to do. . . . I was wanting to come in [and testify] and they was telling me not to. . . . They said, "Don't sue them," and stuff like that, but I feel like, you know, my kids' father was killed up there and they need stuff to get by on with and everything, you know, stuff like that.

She broke down and wept often, particularly when Blue Diamond's lawyer kept asking her about a scrapbook of newspaper clippings about the explosion that someone had sent her, or why her house had burned down a year after the explosion. I was incensed by their tactics, which provided no evidence for the trial but were excruciatingly painful for Geraldine, and for me as I had to watch her suffer through this unnecessary ordeal. I tried to help her by objecting to many of their questions, and I called for numerous breaks in the deposition to help her regain her composure. But I still felt helpless to fully protect her. She testified she had become very nervous since the explosion, and had visited a doctor often to help her deal with her nerves. These were difficult times for her, but she made it through her deposition.

Tragically, before the second anniversary of her husband's death, Geraldine Coots committed suicide. I wish I could have done more to protect her and worry that I might have contributed to her suffering by persuading her to pursue her lawsuit. Her suicide haunts me.

# CHAPTER 7

# "Oh God for One More Breath"

After a few months of depositions, written interrogatories, and document discovery by each side, Blue Diamond filed a summary judgment motion to dismiss our case, arguing that since the facts undisputedly proved that Blue Diamond and Scotia were one company, Blue Diamond was entitled to share in Scotia's workers' compensation immunity from a lawsuit. We, of course, argued to the contrary, that the facts proved they were separate companies, so only Scotia, and not Blue Diamond, was entitled to immunity. Judge Hermansdorfer did not rule on the motion. Instead, six weeks before our jury trial was to commence, he "passed it to the merits," whatever that meant. Maybe, since he had assured Judge Taylor we would have an early trial if our case was transferred out of Tennessee, he meant he was not going to dismiss our case before we had our promised trial.

At the trial we intended to seek compensation for

the lost earnings of each of the men, punitive damages for Blue Diamond's recklessness, and damages for the pain and suffering of the six men who did not die immediately. There are numerous cases holding that the estates of people who die in airplane crashes may recover damages for the physical and emotional pain and suffering of those trapped in the airplane for those last few seconds or minutes as the plane spirals to the ground. We would argue that these six miners suffered the most excruciating psychic as well as bodily pain for at least an hour before their self-rescuers gave out, unable to talk with the self-rescuers in their mouths, probably communicating only by nods and gestures and the looks in their eyes, suffering from the conscious horror of their impending deaths, knowing they were leaving their wives and parents and thinking of their young children who would have to grow up without their fathers.

We will never know exactly what went through the minds of the six Scotia miners behind their barricade in the last hours and minutes of their lives, but we do know what other trapped miners have felt in earlier coal mine explosions. More than one hundred years ago, at the Fraterville coal mine explosion near Coal Creek, Tennessee, 184 men and boys died. When the rescuers finally reached the bodies, they found a barricade had been placed across an entry deep in the mine to try to protect twenty-six miners found there. They left a few notes. Harry Beech wrote a few times to his wife, Alice, and his daughter, Ellen, as he and his friends lay dying, gasping for breath:

> Alice, do the best you can. I am going to rest. Goodbye Alice . . . Do the best you can with the children. We are all perishing for air to support us. But it is getting so bad without any air.
>
> It is now 1-1/2 o'clock [five hours and fifty minutes after the explosion] . . . Raise the children the best way you can. Oh how I would love to be with you. Goodbye to all of you. Bury me and El-bert [another miner trapped with him] in the same grave. Tell little Ellen goodbye. Goodbye Ellen . . . We are together.
>
> It is now 25 minutes after 2 o'clock [six hours and forty-five minutes after the explosion]. A few of us are alive yet, Jacob and Elbert. OH GOD FOR ONE MORE BREATH. Ellen, remember me as long as you live.

At Scotia it took about thirteen hours for the rescue teams to reach the six miners behind their makeshift barricade. The dead men left no notes, but there was other evidence that they had suffered greatly. Self-rescuers become uncomfortably hot when they have to filter large concentrations of carbon monoxide from the air. A few of the men were found with their opened self-rescuers lying next to them. The coroner would testify that "their lips were blistered" and parched, indicating they had worn the self-rescuers until they could no longer stand the searing heat. Their bodies were discolored, evidence that they had died from the carbon monoxide poisoning that filled the mine after the explosion. We wanted to recover for their suffering in their last hours.

# CHAPTER 8

# "A Deferred Victory"

John Adams wrote in the Massachusetts constitution that we should aspire to "be a government of laws and not of men." His fine sentiment has been quoted with approval by the United States Supreme Court and every state supreme court. But laws are administered by men, and as we saw with Judge Taylor, men have feelings. That helped us with Judge Taylor. Things would be remarkably different with Judge Hermansdorfer, who seemed wholly unsympathetic to the widows' lawsuit.

Blue Diamond filed a motion to preclude any recovery for the pain and suffering of the six miners, arguing that we had to choose under Kentucky law between a lawsuit for their pain and suffering and a lawsuit for the loss of their earning power had they lived. We quickly found that, on the contrary, the Kentucky legislature specifically allowed a decedent's estate to sue both for the pain and suffering of the decedent and for the loss of the decedent's earning power. Blue Diamond withdrew its meritless motion. Now we hoped we could introduce testimony about the suffering of the six men, testimony which might make the jury more sympathetic to the Scotia widows and their lawsuit.

On the eve of trial, Judge Hermansdorfer found another way to keep the jury from hearing evidence about the pain and suffering of the six miners. On his own motion and over our strenuous objection, he decided the trial would be bifurcated. This meant that the issue of whether Blue Diamond caused the explosion would be tried first and separately from a second trial on the issue of the damages if, and only if, Blue Diamond was found liable in the first trial. In that initial liability trial the jury would not hear anything about the miners' suffering, since that would be relevant only to compensation if there was a need for a later damages trial. And the jury in the first trial would also not hear any testimony from the Scotia widows, since they had no knowledge relevant to the cause of the explosion. We would have a trial, as Judge Hermansdorfer had promised, but the initial liability trial would be shorn of sympathy.

Judge Hermansdorfer was not through. We planned to prove that the Scotia mine explosion was caused by a buildup of unventilated methane gas to a volatile level between 5 and 15 percent in the air in the Two Southeast Mains section of the mine. Why was it unventilated? Because Blue Diamond had ordered the men to pull back eighteen hundred feet from the end of Two Southeast Mains, where they had been mining, and to start a new mining section off to the left of Two Southeast Mains to be called Two Left off Two Southeast Mains. To turn in to Two Left required the removal of two concrete ventilation stoppings that had directed air to the end of Two Southeast Mains. Without those stoppings, the air short-circuited into Two Left, where the men now would be working, without first sweeping the methane out of the end of the temporarily idled Two Southeast Mains section.

Once those two ventilation stoppings were removed, Blue Diamond should have built permanent ventilation overcasts at the intersection of Two Southeast Mains and Two Left to split the air into two currents, one on top to continue funneling fresh air into Two Southeast Mains with another underneath to provide air to Two Left. Instead, Blue Diamond ordered the immediate mining of the new Two Left section eighteen hundred feet back from the face of Two Southeast Mains before the construction of the overcasts was completed. Blue Diamond also hid from MESA these ventilation changes at the intersection of Two Southeast Mains and Two

Left, when Blue Diamond's engineer falsely certified that those two concrete stoppings were still in place on the ventilation map provided to MESA just before the explosion.

The last words heard from any of the fifteen men before the explosion were those of Geraldine Coots's husband, Virgil, the foreman bossing a crew of twelve men who were mining coal six hundred feet back into the new Two Left section. He called the ventilation boss on the mine telephone to say, "You've cut off all my air." When matters did not improve, he called again a few minutes later to say, "I'm not getting any air. I'm coming down to see what the problem is." That meant he was leaving the end of Two Left to walk about six hundred feet back to the intersection of Two Left and Two Southeast Mains. The mine exploded before he reached that intersection.

Why did it explode? Without the required concrete ventilation stoppings at the intersection, methane accumulated beyond 15 percent of the air in the temporarily unused Two Southeast Mains section. At levels above 15 percent, the methane was not combustible. At about the same time that Virgil Coots realized he had lost air in Two Left, two miners were driving two seven-ton locomotives, hooked in tandem and pushing a load of steel rails, through the intersection. They were headed up to the end of Two Southeast Mains to bring new rail to be laid there for a new, taller coal-mining machine. They probably brought fresh air rushing with them into Two Southeast Mains and away from Two Left as they drove through the intersection. In doing so, they inadvertently diluted the methane in Two Southeast Mains down from above 15 percent to the combustible level between 5 and 15 percent. Almost immediately, this explosive mixture was ignited, probably by a spark from their battery-operated locomotive.

We assumed this was what the extensive MESA "Report of the Scotia Mine Disaster" would say about the cause of the explosion. This MESA report, about to be released, would form the foundation for our whole case. Indeed, a week before the trial we informed Blue Diamond and the court that our first expert witness to prove the cause of the explosion would be the author of the forthcoming MESA report.

But Blue Diamond had an ace up its sleeve. That same week, Blue Diamond filed a separate lawsuit against the secretary of the interior to restrain MESA from publishing its report. Blue Diamond alleged, among other things, that MESA was biased against Blue

Diamond, and further, that because the MESA investigators had talked with me, the independence of the government's report was compromised. This litigation was brought before Judge Hermansdorfer, who held a hearing and quickly decided, five days before our trial was to begin, that a MESA official showed "putative bias" in the preparation of the report. He then ordered the MESA report sealed until he "had the opportunity to examine the report *in camera* [in secret] to determine whether or not the report is prejudicial to any portion of the [Blue Diamond] litigation now pending and assigned for trial. . . ."

Of course the MESA report was "prejudicial" to Blue Diamond, since the purpose of the report was to determine the cause of the explosion, and everyone assumed it would conclude that the unventilated methane gas in Two Southeast Mains had been the cause of the explosion, once it was ignited. The MESA investigators had questioned everyone they could about the Scotia mine explosion. I assumed they had talked with Blue Diamond's lawyers and mining experts. The fact that they had also talked to me was irrelevant to the independence of the MESA report. Moreover, under the Federal Rules of Evidence, Judge Hermansdorfer could keep just the "unduly" prejudicial portions of the report from the jury if he wanted to. But he went way beyond that. He sealed the entire MESA report until he could study it. He wrapped his demoralizing decision in the cloak of high-minded principle:

> I think it's very important when an agency of the United States deals with the public that they be like Caesar's wife, not only above reproach, but giving the appearance of being above reproach.

We will see how scrupulously he applied that maxim to himself.

I was distraught. We had lost our right to introduce the best and most comprehensive expert evidence of the cause of the Scotia explosion. Never before had any MESA report on the cause of a coal mine accident been suppressed. I was in way over my head. I could not see how we could now present sworn testimony to convince a jury, and certainly not Judge Hermansdorfer, that Blue Diamond was liable for the Scotia explosion. I was anxious and depressed, but somehow we still had to present our case in less than a week. At this late date we were prohibited from adding any new expert witnesses to the trial witness list we had already exchanged with Blue Diamond, so we scrambled frantically to persuade one of the fact witnesses on our previously disclosed witness list to testify also as an expert about the probable cause of the explosion. We assumed Judge Hermansdorfer would prohibit testimony from any such previously undisclosed expert, but we tried anyway. We had no choice.

The weekend before the trial in Pikeville, our legal team stayed at the Jenny Wiley State Park Lodge, about twenty-five miles away. That weekend I paced like a caged lion, practicing my opening statement in an empty amphitheater in the park. I tried to calm my nerves by reading a book about my hero, the celebrated trial lawyer Clarence Darrow, trying cases in various towns around the United States, representing the underdog against the local entrenched interests. I was fighting on behalf of the Scotia widows who were taking on Big Daddy Coal, the most powerful interest in Eastern Kentucky, against the wishes of many of their friends and families. So now I was Clarence Darrow? Or maybe I was Mighty Mouse, declaring, "Here I come to save the day!" I roller-coasted from depression to grandiosity. Then I hit reality. I was confronted by the larger-than-life-size portrait of Bert Combs in the lodge's lobby and felt like an overwhelmed outsider once again.

When the Scotia women and their lawyers arrived at the federal courthouse at the end of Main Street in Pikeville, Kentucky, for the opening of the trial, Judge Hermansdorfer had more unpleasant surprises for us. Traditionally the plaintiffs and their counsel are seated closest to the jury box. Instead, Judge Hermansdorfer placed Bert Combs and his team next to the jury and relegated the Scotia women and their lawyers to the far side of the courtroom. He explained that he did this because there were so many plaintiffs, and it would be too crowded for them to sit near the jury. Bert Combs then effectively used his place next to the jury. He wore mismatched coat and pants, with a cigarette burn on the coat sleeve closest to the jury, showing him to be a man of the people and not the wealthy coal company lawyer he had now become. And from his seat just a few feet from the jury, he often whispered under his breath loud enough for the jury to hear his derogatory views of our witnesses' testimony.

When we picked the six-person jury, the number allowed under the Federal Rules of Civil Procedure, we tried to avoid people partial to Bert Combs or to coal operators. We had retained a local plaintiff's lawyer in Pikeville, Kentucky, to try to limit Bert Combs's power, but it was a daunting, uphill fight. After each side exhausted its right to exclude some of the potential jurors, a jury of six persons was seated in the jury box:

1. A factory worker whose husband was a teacher—they had one child working for a coal company
2. A housewife whose husband was a disabled coal miner
3. A lunchroom aide at an elementary school with a husband in coal strip mining
4. A twenty-three-year-old security guard at a government depot
5. A cook at an elementary school whose husband had retired from the electrical business
6. A housewife whose husband was a teacher—they had a son working in the mines

   1st alternate: a teacher named Combs (not related to Bert Combs—the name Combs was quite common in Eastern Kentucky)

   2nd alternate: a truck driver who was once sued for killing a child in an accident

   3rd alternate: an assistant school principal whose father had severe black lung disease from his days mining coal

Now it was time for my opening statement to the jury. Since Judge Hermansdorfer had temporarily prohibited publication of the MESA report until he could "examine" it, I had to skirt around telling the jury exactly what evidence we would present at the trial on the cause of the explosion. Still, despite Bert Combs's many unusual objections and interruptions during my opening statement, I believed I was able to inform the jury that the evidence would prove Blue Diamond was liable for the Scotia mine explosion because its executives had created an unsafe mining condition in an improperly ventilated gassy coal mine.

Immediately after I completed my opening statement, Bert Combs, to whom Judge Hermansdorfer referred in front of the jury as "Judge Combs" because he had been a judge on both Kentucky's highest court and the Sixth Circuit, rose to try once again to have our case dismissed. He asked Judge Hermansdorfer to instruct the jury peremptorily to find for Blue Diamond, because I had not stated a case on the *proximate cause* of the explosion or the *foreseeability* of the explosion. Of course, the MESA report determined the proximate cause and foreseeability of the explosion, but Judge Hermansdorfer had admonished me not to refer to the MESA report.

Judge Hermansdorfer excused the jury, and we then

· · · 72 · · ·

argued Mr. Combs's motion. Bert Combs admitted he had no cases to cite to Judge Hermansdorfer to support his motion, but he insisted everyone in Kentucky knew you had to state proximate cause in your opening statement. Judge Hermansdorfer joined in: "I did not see in your opening statement any proximate cause statement." My confidence was shattered. I was afraid I had committed some egregious error before I could even present our case to the jury, weak as that case might be without the MESA report. I replied: "Your Honor, the proximate cause as we set forth in the opening statement is that they created a dangerous condition, a dangerous condition of a methane explosion occurred; they did not make certain that the methane, which they knew was accumulating in Two Southeast Mains, was ventilated. As I indicated, that was a dangerous condition that they knew they were creating, and one they did not make certain did not cause an explosion."

Judge Hermansdorfer condescendingly responded, "I think you are saying it now, but I don't know that you said it in your opening statement, Mr. Stern, and in a common-law jurisdiction that's the risk you run." So I pleaded with Judge Hermansdorfer, "I would like to be given the opportunity, then, if you didn't feel that I stated what I now state to you, to state that to the jury."

No way, said Judge Hermansdorfer: "I think it is a little too late, Mr. Stern. I didn't make these rules. They have been in existence for a long time."

He said he would hear argument on "Judge Combs's" motion at four o'clock that afternoon, and told us to bring whatever legal authority we had to that hearing. My associates, George Frampton and Jonathan Schiller, spent the rest of the day frenetically poring through Kentucky law at a local lawyer's office, while I had to begin the presentation of our evidence to the jury without their courtroom assistance, and wondered throughout the day whether our case would be dismissed that afternoon. I was an emotional wreck, but we carried on.

Our first witness was Gordon Bonnyman, Blue Diamond's chairman of the board, president, and largest shareholder. Mr. Bonnyman had graduated from Princeton University, just like Judge Hermansdorfer. Mr. Bonnyman had a civil engineering degree, but denied that he was qualified to testify as to whether methane gas was odorless, or invisible, or tasteless. He did know methane was combustible when it reached levels of 5 to 15 percent of the atmosphere. He knew the Scotia mine was classified as a gassy mine, but he did not know it was one of the gassiest mines in Eastern Kentucky. Still, we offered into evidence, through Mr. Bonnyman, an engineering study he had ordered after the explosion to determine its cause. The assumption from the study was that the explosion occurred when methane built up at the place of ventilation interruption in the mine where two concrete stoppings had been removed.

I also tried to prove through Mr. Bonnyman that Blue Diamond and Scotia were separate corporations, with separate employees, and that Blue Diamond made safety and ventilation decisions for the Scotia mine, including the decisions to remove the two concrete ventilation stoppings and to continue to mine coal before the permanent ventilation changes were completed. Of course he kept trying to testify that Blue Diamond and Scotia were one company.

In the midst of Mr. Bonnyman's testimony, Judge Hermansdorfer interjected a question which baffled me at the time: "Let me ask you a question, Mr. Bonnyman. Who owns the real estate in Letcher County that is occupied by the Scotia Coal Company?" Only later would I understand why Judge Hermansdorfer asked this strange question.

I tried to mark as exhibits five years of net income figures that Blue Diamond had finally produced for me, under seal, for the Blue Diamond Coal Company and the separate Scotia Coal Company. I wanted these exhibits admitted as evidence to show the separate nature of the companies, and also to let the jury know how much money these companies had made by operating their mines without proper safety precautions. Judge Hermansdorfer refused to allow me to mark them or to put them in evidence. He said, "I think they are totally irrelevant. I think they are privileged; they have nothing to do with this lawsuit. It does not matter whether a tortfeasor is wealthy or poor. . . . Kentucky has never held that a rich man has one set of liability standards and a poor man has another, and that's all these figures amount to."

It was comforting to know that the poor man and the rich man had the same rights in Judge Hermansdorfer's court, although I did not see a lot of evidence of that. He then ordered me to return the financial records to Blue Diamond. He would not even allow me to mark them for the record so an appellate court could see them if we ever decided to appeal.

At the end of the day, George Frampton and Jonathan Schiller presented to Judge Hermansdorfer several Kentucky state court decisions which unequivocally held that a directed verdict, after a plaintiff's opening statement, is never based on mere insufficiency of the opening statement to state a case. Kentucky law also allows the plaintiff's lawyer to correct a mistaken opening statement by recalling the jury before the court grants a directed verdict. So there was no basis for Mr. Combs's motion or Judge Hermansdorfer's alleged knowledge of contrary Kentucky rules "in existence for a long time." They did not exist.

Pressing a different point, Judge Hermansdorfer asked about my admission that I did not know what caused the explosion. I replied that my actual words had been that we had no eyewitness to what had happened, but I had said the cause of this particular explosion was the unventilated accumulation of methane gas. I added that I also hoped to have expert testimony through the MESA report that the unventilated methane probably was ignited by a spark from the locomotive.

This infuriated Judge Hermansdorfer: "Let me tell you, Mr. Stern, that you just violated one of the rules I put down . . . and that is no counsel would refer to that report until I ruled on it." After more heated back-and-forth about the still unpublished MESA report, Judge Hermansdorfer came up with another argument. Scotia had a "nondelegable employer's duty to provide a safe place to work . . . so if Blue Diamond, in your theory, had the duty of providing a safe place to work, then you may have eliminated the possibility of recovery." My simple answer was that both had a duty to provide adequate ventilation of the mine.

Judge Hermansdorfer finally gave up, saying, "We are going too far and it is probably my fault. . . . I am going to overrule your motion, Judge Combs, for a directed verdict based on the adequacy of the opening statement." A small victory for mankind, although he had no choice under Kentucky law.

After our hearing, Judge Hermansdorfer held a hearing in the separate case Blue Diamond had earlier filed against the United States to prohibit the publication of the MESA report. In that case, Judge Hermansdorfer had temporarily ordered the government not to publish the report until he had an "opportunity to examine" it. He had now had the time to review it, so the United States filed a motion to allow MESA to publish it. MESA was required to investigate all serious coal mine accidents, determine the causes of those accidents, and then report to the public their findings and conclusions, particularly so coal mine operators would be educated on how to prevent any similar future accidents. Never before had MESA been prohibited from publishing an investigative report, so MESA was eager to have

Judge Hermansdorfer lift his temporary order prohibiting that publication.

We were hopeful that the government would be able to convince Judge Hermansdorfer how important it was for the public to have access to this MESA report. Of course, if the government were to prevail, we then could use the MESA report in our case.

Judge Hermansdorfer heard testimony from witnesses explaining how the investigation was undertaken and how the report was prepared. Blue Diamond then argued that MESA was biased against Blue Diamond because MESA wanted the report to show that Blue Diamond, and not MESA, was responsible for both of the Scotia explosions. There was some basis for this argument as to the second Scotia explosion, which occurred when MESA was in charge of the mine and was beginning its investigation of the first explosion. For that second explosion it was clearly in MESA's interest to deny its responsibility and instead place the blame on Blue Diamond. But there was no legitimate basis for arguing that MESA was responsible for the first explosion. Nevertheless, Judge Hermansdorfer quickly reaffirmed his order to prohibit publication of all, or any part, of the MESA report.

We would have to complete the presentation of our

case against Blue Diamond without any access to the basic facts and expert opinions in the MESA report. We went back to our local lawyer's office to prepare for the next day, but we could not concentrate. We could not get past the thrashing we had taken that first day. Tempers flared. My associate, Jonathan Schiller, was outraged at the way Judge Hermansdorfer had treated us, and even angrier at me for so calmly taking a beating from him. He admonished me that the judge was destroying our case, and I was not doing anything about it. I was furious too, but I thought we had no choice but to keep pressing forward despite Judge Hermansdorfer's obvious efforts to undermine our case. I tried to remind Jonathan that I had spent two years trying voting rights cases in the South before hostile, racist judges just as difficult as Judge Hermansdorfer. I had been taught that the only thing to do with a hostile judge was to make sure you created a clear and complete record of sworn testimony and exhibits for the inevitable appeal to the Court of Appeals. This was now our job: Even without the MESA report, we had to make a record proving Blue Diamond's liability for the explosion, a record that could withstand a motion for a directed verdict at the close of our testimony and that would incense an appellate court if we lost. That is exactly what we attempted to do.

The next day we tried in various ways to introduce expert testimony from our previously designated fact witnesses, but Blue Diamond and Judge Hermansdorfer effectively blocked us. For example, I tried to make an expert of Rick Keene, a former MESA ventilation inspection engineer we had listed in the earlier pretrial order only as a fact witness, when we still assumed we would have the MESA report and its author as our expert witness. But when I attempted to have Mr. Keene give his opinion on whether it would have been a safe condition to remove the two concrete stoppings shown on the approved ventilation plan and replace them with plastic curtains, Blue Diamond objected because we had not previously listed Mr. Keene as an expert witness. Judge Hermansdorfer had no trouble with that one. He loved telling me I had to play by the rules.

Blue Diamond's counsel had no cross-examination questions for Mr. Keene and told him he could step down from the witness box. To everyone's surprise, Judge Hermansdorfer immediately interjected that he had some questions. I assumed he thought Mr. Keene's testimony, truncated as it was, still was too helpful to the plaintiffs' case, and he thought Blue Diamond should have cross-examined him to deflate his testimony. So he did it himself. He led Mr. Keene to admit that each ventilation plan submitted on the Scotia mine showed that the ventilation at that mine was adequate under the MESA regulations, that Mr. Keene had never closed the mine because of inadequate ventilation, that he had never found anything that made the mine unsafe for coal miners as far as ventilation was concerned, that any safety violations would be served only on the Scotia Coal Company, and that he had never cited Blue Diamond Coal Company for any safety violations. The judge had pretty much undermined our case, particularly by leaving the impression from his questions that Mr. Keene thought the mine ventilation was safe.

I tried to rehabilitate our case by requestioning Mr. Keene to emphasize that his testimony about the safety of the mine was based only on the ventilation maps he had been shown just before the explosion and that those maps falsely identified concrete stoppings that had in fact been removed and replaced by temporary plastic curtains. But again I was not allowed to continue further and have Mr. Keene testify to his expert opinion that mining with temporary plastic curtains instead of permanent concrete stoppings made for an unsafe condition.

I argued that Judge Hermansdorfer himself had opened up the issue of the safety of the mine by his own questions of Mr. Keene, so the plaintiffs should have been allowed to respond by asking Mr. Keene his expert opinion on safety. Eventually, at the end of the day, after Mr. Keene had been dismissed as a witness, Judge Hermansdorfer recognized he had gone too far and finally agreed that, because he had asked Mr. Keene for his opinion on a safety issue, we too were entitled to ask his expert opinion on the safety of removing the concrete stoppings. Rather than recall Mr. Keene to testify, Blue Diamond agreed to a stipulation that we would read to the jury the next day:

It is stipulated by the parties that if Mr. Keene were asked the following question he would give the following answer: Assuming the approved ventilation plan in effect at the time and its requirements; and further assuming that two stoppings had been removed at the intersection of Two Southeast Mains and Two Left and had been replaced by plastic curtains, can you form an opinion as to whether that would be a safe condition? Answer. Yes. What is that opinion? In my opinion it would not be a safe condition.

We had weathered another difficult, infuriating day. We had even introduced into evidence an expert opinion on the unsafe conditions created at the Scotia mine.

Each night, after the trial adjourned for the day, I talked with the women. They were despondent. They had been in the courtroom during the trial and had seen Judge Hermansdorfer's open antipathy to their case. This was not the lawsuit they had envisioned. No one was breaking down on the witness stand and admitting that Blue Diamond had recklessly killed fifteen coal miners. No one was apologizing to them for putting Blue Diamond's profits ahead of the safety of their husbands. They were not being allowed to vent their anger on Blue Diamond's executives in open court. Still, I tried to assure them that all was not lost. We had prevailed in the arguments before Judge Hermansdorfer at the end of each of the first two days. And if we could get our case submitted to the jury, I thought we had enough evidence, even without the MESA report, to persuade them of Blue Diamond's liability. The jury was our best, and only, hope.

We reviewed our case, determining what we had proved so far and what we had left to prove on the issue of Blue Diamond's liability. Without the MESA report we were fast running out of witnesses, though we still had some additional evidence to offer. We had a few minor witnesses testify the next day and then tried to mark and offer the MESA report into evidence. Judge Hermansdorfer would not let us do so. Instead, he ordered us to return to the government our copies of the draft MESA report, which we had been provided as part of the earlier injunction proceeding against the government. We had no more evidence to present to prove Blue Diamond's liability for the explosion, so we rested our case on a Friday afternoon.

Blue Diamond immediately moved for a directed verdict because of our alleged failure to prove the proximate cause of the explosion. It also renewed its earlier motion for summary judgment on the Kentucky workers' compensation immunity issue, the motion Judge Hermansdorfer had not ruled on prior to the trial. Judge Hermansdorfer heard the beginning of Bert Combs's arguments in support of his motions and then recessed for the day and ordered both sides to return Monday morning with citations to legal cases to support their positions.

That weekend we spent a dreary few days at Jenny Wiley State Park. My wife and two young sons flew down from Washington to be with us, but I was terrible company. George, Jonathan, and I combed over the case law and the facts we had proved. We believed we had introduced into evidence enough expert testimony on the cause of the explosion so Judge Hermansdorfer could not dismiss our case on the proximate cause of the explosion. We also thought we had proved that Blue Diamond and Scotia were separate companies, so Blue Diamond would not be entitled to shelter under Scotia's immunity from suit. At any rate, the issue of immunity under Kentucky's workers' compensation statute was part of Blue Diamond's affirmative defense, so we were hoping the judge would want to hear the testimony in Blue Diamond's defense case before deciding that issue.

We returned with the Scotia women to the court on Monday morning with a lengthy memorandum on proximate cause that George Frampton and Jonathan Schiller had prepared that weekend in opposition to Blue Diamond's motion for a directed verdict. But the argument quickly turned to Blue Diamond's pretrial motion for summary judgment under the immunity granted by Kentucky's workers' compensation statute. The argument went badly for us. Blue Diamond and the judge were now focused on the words of the Kentucky workers' compensation statute that required a "contractor" to provide workers' compensation payments to employees of any company they contract with to do work for them. In exchange, such contractors are given immunity from lawsuits. This new argument conceded that Blue Diamond and Scotia were not "one ball of wax." Instead, now they were separate companies, and Blue Diamond was a "contractor" which had contracted with Scotia to mine coal for Blue Diamond. In this new scenario, Blue Diamond was the "contractor" directly responsible to pay workers' compensation for Scotia's employees, and therefore also directly immune from lawsuit under Kentucky law.

This argument was fatally flawed because there was no such contract. Moreover, the coal was mined for Scotia and not for Blue Diamond, and the proceeds from the sale of the coal were Scotia's. Finally, Scotia, not Blue Diamond, paid the workers' compensation. Judge Hermansdorfer was not deterred. He held there was an "implied contract" between Blue Diamond and Scotia, Blue Diamond was a "contractor," and Blue Diamond, therefore, was immune from suit under Kentucky law. "Reluctantly," so he claimed, he granted Blue Diamond's summary judgment motion and "set aside the swearing of the jury." Blue Diamond would not have to put on any defense witnesses, and the widows would not get the chance to have a jury decide their case. We were out of court, a year and three months after the Scotia mine explosion.

We trudged dejectedly back up Main Street in Pikeville, from the courthouse to the second floor office of our local lawyer, Kelsey Friend. We were beaten and depressed. The women were crying. Jennifer Boggs summed it up: "Well, I guess that's it." It was hard to put a happy spin on this terrible blow, but I tried. I said it might not be over yet. At least we now had a ruling on the workers' compensation immunity issue, and we always knew that whoever lost on that issue would want to appeal to the Sixth Circuit. Still, I would have preferred to go there the winner defending a lower court victory instead of the loser trying to reverse the lower court. We shed some tears ourselves, and then called my partners, Mitch Rogovin and Harry Huge, back in Washington, to tell them the shocking news that we would not be allowed to have a jury decide our case. We had lost. We discussed whether our law firm had the will and financial ability to proceed with an appeal. Mitch listened to our despair and sadness, and then he brightened our mood: "This is not a defeat, it is a deferred victory." These were the comforting, hopeful words we needed to hear.

We packed our bags and wearily headed back home. By this time we had devoted hundreds of thousands of dollars' worth of lawyers' time to this case, and expended thousands of out-of-pocket dollars for expenses. An appeal was a long shot, and would take at least a few years more of our legal time and our cash. Nevertheless, we intended to try. In the meantime, Sally Maggard and Dan Hendrickson, the volunteers from the Council of Southern Mountains, would keep the women's spirits up while we toiled away on the appeal.

# CHAPTER 9

# All or Nothing

To move our appeal along faster in the Court of Appeals we filed a motion for an expedited oral argument. Our motion was granted, though no argument date was set. A few months later I called Bert Combs about settling the case. I felt I owed it to the women to get the best offer I could for them before the oral argument. If that argument indicated the judges were not willing to overrule Judge Hermansdorfer, their case really would be over. Bert Combs agreed to meet with me on one of his next trips to Washington.

When we met, he told me I was "trying to thread the needle" with my legal argument, and cautioned me that my chances on appeal to his old court were not good. He reminded me that one of Blue Diamond's attorneys had informed Kelsey Friend, our local counsel in Pikeville, that Blue Diamond had been willing to hear an offer to settle with each woman, before trial, for twenty-five thousand dollars plus the workers' compensation checks each had been receiving. Mr. Combs said Blue Diamond at that point had even had authority to go as high as fifty thousand dollars for each woman, if the women had made such an offer to settle. However, now that Judge Hermansdorfer had dismissed our case, Blue Diamond was willing to offer each of the women only ten thousand dollars and the right to keep her workers' compensation payments. This offer was conditioned on agreement by all of the women.

Mr. Combs clearly believed Blue Diamond was in the driver's seat, so the offer was meant to pressure the widows into a quick settlement, before the Sixth Circuit oral argument. They had had a chance at twenty-five thousand or maybe even fifty thousand, but now the offer was ten thousand, and if they passed that up, the next offer might be even lower. I told him I was certain the women would refuse, but I was required by the rules of ethics to forward the offer to them.

The women responded. Jennifer Boggs wrote: "I would not settle for $10,000, $25,000, or $50,000. What do they think the value of a human life is? I would rather have nothing from them. We have gone through too much to stop now." Debbie Turner wrote: "I say no way. Not for me." Diana McKnight wrote: "It sure was an insult. David made more than that the last year he worked. That's not even enough to pay off my bills. Nor would it be enough to help keep Melissa in school. I would like to get enough to be able to give her a good education. I'd just like to know who they think they are anyway. . . . For me I lost a brother and a husband. They'll never replace them in our hearts. And they act like it would kill them to give us what we deserve to raise our kids and live. Well I close. I guess I've said enough. But not half of what I'd like to tell them. And it would give me the most pleasure to tell them to their face." Fortunately, the company's insistence on all or nothing meant that the one woman who wanted to settle for ten thousand dollars could not. And maybe someday Diana McKnight would get her chance to "tell them to their face" how she felt.

The offer was not a good one for our fledgling law firm either. I kept a running tabulation in my desk drawer of the total hours our law firm spent on this case. Those hours multiplied by our hourly rates totaled what we would have earned if we had been working on paying cases. I watched in horror as the fees we could have earned, plus the expenses we had paid out, mounted to the point that I wondered whether we could break even, even if we did win the case. At ten thousand dollars per plaintiff, their total recovery would be one hundred fifty thousand dollars, which would only cover our out-of-pocket expenses, pay us a small fraction of the fees we could have earned for the hours we spent on the case, and leave the women with less than one hundred thousand dollars to be split among the fifteen families. The women and our law firm had a lot riding on the appeal. My partners also were anxious about the outcome, and wanted me back working on paying cases as soon as possible.

A few days after I met with Bert Combs in Washington, the Sixth Circuit scheduled our expedited oral argument for June 1978 in Cincinnati, nine months after Judge Hermansdorfer had dismissed our case. Six days before that oral argument, Bert Combs called with a new offer, twenty-five thousand dollars per woman. Two days later he called again to emphasize that the offer was available only if all the women accepted before eight in the morning on the day of the oral argument. He chose that time because that was when Blue Diamond and the plaintiffs would learn for the first time the names of the three judges who would hear the appeal. There are numerous judges on the Sixth Circuit, but each case is decided by only a three-judge panel, and until the day of the argument the lawyers do not know which three judges will be assigned to their case. We never responded to the all-or-nothing twenty-five-thousand-dollar settlement offer, since at least one woman, Jennifer Boggs, had already said she would never settle for that amount of money.

The night before the oral argument I nervously paced the floor of my hotel room in Cincinnati, constantly changing the first lines of my oral argument. I assumed I would not get much beyond those first lines before the judges started peppering me with hard questions. I knew our case was a big gamble, but I also thought that if the judges read the transcript of the trial, which we had attached to the appendix of exhibits that the Sixth Circuit had before them, they could not help feeling the widows had not been treated fairly.

Early the next morning we learned that our panel would include two senior circuit judges: Lester Cecil, President Eisenhower's first judicial appointment, and John Peck, a Democrat like Judge Combs. Both Judge Peck, who would be the chief judge of our panel, and Judge Cecil had served alongside Judge Combs for the four years Judge Combs had served as a Sixth Circuit judge. The third judge was a newer circuit judge, Gilbert Merritt, from Nashville. I was relieved to see Judge Merritt's name.

Before President Carter appointed Judge Merritt to
the bench, he had practiced law in Nashville and had
even done pro bono work for a citizens' group protest-
ing the low tax assessment of coal land in Tennessee. He
also was a longtime friend of John Seigenthaler, Sr., then
the publisher of the Nashville *Tennessean*. I knew John
from my days in the Civil Rights Division of the United
States Department of Justice, when I was just out of law
school and working on voting rights cases in the early
1960s in the South, and he was the administrative assistant to Attorney General Robert Kennedy. Our law firm
had also worked with another of Judge Merritt's best
friends, Jim Neal, a well-known Nashville trial attorney.
Jim Neal had been one of the Watergate prosecutors,
and one of his young protégés was George Frampton,
the lawyer in our firm who worked on the Scotia trial
and on our appellate brief. Jim Neal also was listed as
Of Counsel to our Rogovin, Stern and Huge law firm.
We were not completely without friends in Judge
Combs's former court.

Nevertheless, I felt we were on Combs's home terri-
tory once again. When I stood up to make our oral argument, Bert Combs kept interrupting me, as though he
was still a member of the court entitled to question me
while I was making my argument. It is most unusual for

counsel to interrupt while the other side's lawyer is making his or her argument, but Chief Judge Peck did not admonish him. Judge Peck also seemed unimpressed with our argument, and his questions made it clear he was not interested in overruling Judge Hermansdorfer. Judge Merritt, on the other hand, seemed shocked at the way Judge Hermansdorfer had treated us, and his hard questions to Bert Combs during his reply to our argument offered us some hope. Judge Cecil was mostly uninvolved in the argument, so we could not guess which way he was leaning. When the arguments concluded, the judges gave no indication how they might rule. When we left the courtroom I was shaking, like the man who just put all he owned on number twenty-two on the roulette table. Now the wheel was spinning, and it was all or nothing—go home broke or hit the jackpot.

# CHAPTER 10

# "Like Caesar's Wife"

M onths later, while we were still waiting for the Sixth Circuit to decide our appeal, I received an anonymous call from a lawyer calling from a pay phone in Pikeville, Kentucky. He said he had watched what Judge Hermansdorfer had done to me and the widows during the Scotia trial and was appalled and embarrassed that we had been treated so unfairly. Then he said he wanted me to know that Judge Hermansdorfer owned land on which he received royalties from coal mining, and hung up.

I was stunned. No one, not our local counsel in Pikeville, and none of the young journalists from the Kentucky papers who followed the trial each day and were favorably inclined toward the women, had ever mentioned that Judge Hermansdorfer was receiving royalties from the mining of coal on his own land. Judge Hermansdorfer never offered us this information, and he never asked us whether we thought he should recuse— that is, disqualify—himself from our case on that ground.

Maybe that is why he had asked Mr. Bonnyman the name of the owner of the property "occupied by the Scotia Coal Company." Was Judge Hermansdorfer wondering whether he, as a property owner of land being mined for coal, could be sued if a coal mine disaster occurred on his own land? There was a Kentucky case which held that a landowner could *not* be sued for workers' compensation, so under our theory in the Scotia case that meant a landowner *could* be sued for an accident on his land. Did the judge then wonder whether he, as a landowner, might still have immunity from such a suit under the "contractor" provision if something should go wrong in the mining process? Perhaps finding Blue Diamond immune from suit as a "contractor" would be helpful to him if he ever was sued for a coal mining accident on his own land. He could say he too was immune from suit because he was a "contractor" who had contracted with another company to mine coal for him.

Clearly he should have either recused himself from our case, or informed us of all the facts relating to his coal holdings and coal royalties and let the plaintiffs determine whether to waive their right to disqualify him.

As Judge Hermansdorfer, an agent of the United States, so sanctimoniously had held in sealing the much-needed MESA report: "I think it's very important when an agency of the United States deals with the public that they be like Caesar's wife, not only above reproach, but giving the appearance of being above reproach."

Now we faced a major dilemma. If I took this information to the Court of Appeals before they ruled on the legal issue of workers' compensation immunity, that court might halt its work on our appeal and instead send our case back to Judge Hermansdorfer for him to decide this recusal issue. On the other hand, if we did not inform the Court of Appeals, and they then ruled against us on the immunity issue, the women would have lost their chance to argue that the district judge who decided their case should have disqualified himself. We resolved our quandary by telling the women about the phone call and then taking the information to the press. That way, the judges on our Court of Appeals panel might learn from the news media about Judge Hermansdorfer's coal holdings, and we would not have to file a motion on the recusal issue, which could delay their decision on our immunity issue. Maybe the panel's knowledge of Judge Hermansdorfer's appearance of impropriety also would make them more sympathetic to our case.

I was not planning to do anything illegal, unethical, or even improper, such as leaking any confidential information under seal in the Scotia lawsuit. Still, I momentarily wondered about the wisdom of making a clandestine call to a Kentucky reporter and asking him to keep the fact of my call confidential. A Kentucky reporter might think keeping Bert Combs on his side would be better for his future career than to have me, a Washington outsider, as his secret source. And if word reached Judge Hermansdorfer that I was the person leaking information to the press about him, he could do me great harm, maybe attempt to hold me in contempt of his court. But I had to get the information to the public, and hopefully to the Sixth Circuit.

I also realized that the sparse information I had learned over the phone needed to be more fully investigated before it could be released publicly, and I thought a Kentucky reporter would have much greater ability to get the information than I would. I trusted Bill Bishop, a young reporter from Louisville who had been covering our Scotia case and had written sympathetic stories about the women. So I called and told him what I had heard. He conducted an investigation, and a few weeks later his article appeared in the Louisville *Times* under the headline JUDGE WHO SITS IN COAL CASES GETS ROYALTIES—

HERMANSDORFER, OF U.S. EASTERN DISTRICT, OWNS MIN-
ERAL RIGHTS. He reported that the Paul Coffey Construction Company had been strip mining coal on the
judge's family land near Ashland, Kentucky, since the
year of the Scotia mine explosion. His story added:

> The American Bar Association's Code of Judicial
> Conduct admonishes judges "to refrain from fi-
> nancial and business dealings that tend to reflect
> adversely on (their) impartiality." The Code also
> advises judges to "avoid impropriety and the ap-
> pearance of impropriety in all (their) dealings."
> The Code recommends that a judge disqualify
> himself in "proceedings in which his impartiality
> might be questioned."

Bill Bishop also quoted the chief judge of the United
States Court of Appeals for the Sixth Circuit as saying
he was unaware of Judge Hermansdorfer's coal leases.
The article continued:

> According to some lawyers who have practiced be-
> fore him, Judge Hermansdorfer apparently has not
> made it a general policy to inform those who
> have coal-related cases in his court about his coal

leases. . . . Attorneys for the U.S. Department of Labor and Department of Justice involved in specific coal-related cases before Hermansdorfer, and the lead attorneys who represented survivors of both Scotia and Hyden victims, all said they were not informed by the judge of his interest in the coal business.

Of course, Bert Combs came to Judge Hermansdorfer's defense. He was quoted as saying that Judge Hermansdorfer's coal interests were "common knowledge" among lawyers practicing in the Eastern District, and that such a coal connection "wasn't of significant interest to anybody because most everybody who owns any appreciable amount of land down there owns some coal."

The other Louisville paper, the *Courier-Journal,* printed a follow-up story, perhaps prompted by Bert Combs. This story quoted the president of the Kentucky Bar Association as saying that Judge Hermansdorfer "has a practice in his court of telling everyone of his coal interests." The reporter for this story found that hard to believe, since he knew personally from covering the Scotia trial that no such announcement had been made. The reporter added that during the trial he had interviewed

Judge Hermansdorfer and asked him if he or his family was involved in coal mining. Judge Hermansdorfer had said, "I do not own a coal company. I do not own any stock in a coal company." That clever response did not "tell . . . everyone of his coal interests" and coal mining royalties.

Nothing more happened on the recusal issue until I received a phone call from John Seigenthaler. He had been appointed by President Carter to chair a committee to screen applicants for a vacancy on the United States Court of Appeals for the Sixth Circuit, and Judge Hermansdorfer was on the list of those being considered for a presidential appointment to fill that opening. He wanted to know what I knew about the judge.

I told him I could not discuss Judge Hermansdorfer because our appeal was pending at the Sixth Circuit on his decision against us in the Scotia case. He said he would tell me what his committee had learned, and then ask me if any of what they had collected was, to my knowledge, untrue. He detailed what their committee discovered about Judge Hermansdorfer's treatment of the women's case in the Scotia trial and what they had read about his coal holdings. I had to admit I heard nothing untrue in what John Seigenthaler told me. I later learned his committee put Judge Hermansdorfer at the bottom of their list of the judges being considered for the Sixth Circuit opening. Several committee members told *The Washington Post* that the judge's coal holdings had raised serious concerns about potential conflicts of interest. The committee also had required Judge Hermansdorfer to tell them how much he was earning from the coal being mined on his property. He did, and reportedly it was much more than the seventeen hundred dollars a year he had reported in a judicial filing after the first newspaper story about his coal royalties.

During our long, torturous wait for a decision from the Sixth Circuit, I also spent time fighting with the United States government over its responsibility for the second explosion at the Scotia mine. Gene Goss and two other Kentucky lawyers, representing five of the widows whose husbands died when they volunteered to go into the Scotia mine with the government mining inspectors, had asked me to lead a lawsuit for these five families. The government refused to pay these women any compensation for the deaths of their husbands, arguing that their husbands had "no duty" to enter the mine and that they were negligent in volunteering to do so when they knew that the gassy mine had just exploded. We responded to this callous and outrageous argument, pointing out that MESA was in control of the mine, had asked the men to volunteer, and had authorized them to enter the mine with the MESA investigators. We then awaited a decision on this legal "duty" issue.

# CHAPTER 11

# "The Hawk Is About to Light"

It was now over a year since Judge Hermansdorfer had dismissed the jury in the middle of our trial in Pikeville, and almost three years since the explosion. For the past seven months since the oral argument on our appeal, the women and I apprehensively waited for a decision from the Sixth Circuit. It was a painful time for them, and for me and the other lawyers of my firm. There were numerous phone calls back and forth to Kentucky as we tried to comfort one another through this agonizing period. Then one morning I was walking back to my office in Washington when I saw my secretary come running out the front door of our building, yelling to me and waving a piece of paper. We had won!

In a two-to-one decision, the appeals court held that we could sue Blue Diamond. Judge Merritt wrote the opinion, with Judge Cecil concurring, that Blue Diamond was not a "contractor" with Scotia, because there was no contract, and that since "Blue Diamond and Scotia were separate and distinct corporations," Blue Diamond was not entitled to hide behind Scotia's immunity from suit under Kentucky's workers' compensation statute. He wrote that immunity from suit needed to be narrowly interpreted, in part because Kentucky's workers' compensation payments had remained low and did not adequately compensate injured employees and their families. Judge Peck dissented, finding Blue Diamond immune from suit based on "the long and thoughtful Memorandum Opinion" of Judge Hermansdorfer.

Breathlessly, I called each of the women to tell them we now had Blue Diamond on the run. But Blue Diamond was fighting back. Its counsel immediately petitioned for a rehearing "en banc," which meant a hearing by *all* the judges of the Sixth Circuit sitting together. If the Sixth Circuit granted a rehearing, that would set aside Judge Merritt's opinion. Then we would have to argue anew the immunity issue before all the judges of the Sixth Circuit, and we could win only if a majority of those judges agreed to reverse Judge Hermansdorfer. After further briefing and another nervous wait, the full Sixth Circuit denied an en banc hearing, thereby affirming Judge Merritt's decision ordering that we be given a new trial.

By now almost two years had passed since Judge Hermansdorfer had dashed the women's hopes that a jury would decide their lawsuit. Maybe this time a jury finally would get to rule on their case. Our law firm was as eager as the women to get on to that new trial, since our legal fees for our time on this case, at our regular hourly rates, now totaled over six hundred thousand dollars, and our out-of-pocket expenses exceeded forty thousand dollars. Our small firm had a lot riding on this new trial.

Within three months after the Sixth Circuit issued its mandate that we be given a new trial, Blue Diamond received further bad news. On June 25, 1979, more than three years after the Scotia mine explosion, a United States grand jury in Pikeville, Kentucky, handed down a criminal indictment charging both Blue Diamond and Scotia with six criminal violations of the Federal Mine Safety and Health Act. Scotia's workers' compensation immunity from civil suit did not protect Scotia, or Blue Diamond, from criminal prosecution. Four counts of the criminal indictment charged both companies with a willful failure to comply with the ventilation plan for the Scotia mine and to make required inspections and examinations for potentially explosive concentrations of methane. The other two counts charged them with making knowingly false statements in records required to be maintained with respect to its ventilation and examination practices. No individuals from either company were criminally charged.

Blue Diamond was not that concerned about these new criminal cases, since criminal prosecutions require the government to meet a higher burden of proof—beyond a reasonable doubt—than a civil case, which only requires proof by a preponderance of the evidence—that is, more likely than not to be true. Moreover, even if the two companies eventually were tried and found criminally guilty, the maximum potential penalties for a conviction called for fines totaling only sixty thousand dollars. These criminal cases, which echoed the same allegations we were making against Blue Diamond in our civil case, were assigned to Judge Hermansdorfer for pretrial motions and trial.

Blue Diamond, still hoping to reverse Judge Merritt's opinion in our civil case, had filed a petition for certiorari asking the United States Supreme Court to allow Blue Diamond to appeal from the decision of the Sixth Circuit. This required more briefs from the legal teams for each side, even though Blue Diamond's petition had little chance of success. In cases like ours, the Supreme Court usually allows an appeal from a circuit court's decision only if that decision conflicts with the decision of another circuit court, and there was no such conflict here. Although Blue Diamond's petition was pending at the Supreme Court, the Sixth Circuit's mandate for a new trial remained in effect.

After the Sixth Circuit denied Blue Diamond's en banc motion, Bert Combs had telephoned to graciously congratulate me on our "impressive victory" at the Sixth Circuit. He said they were now ready to talk settlement, but he emphasized that he did not think a jury in Eastern Kentucky would award the women any significant amount of money, even if we could prove that Blue Diamond, rather than Scotia, had somehow caused the mine to explode. He did not offer any settlement amount, though, and instead said one of their lawyers would be calling Gene Goss, our local lawyer in Harlan, Kentucky, to discuss the procedural steps necessary to reach a settlement.

I immediately telephoned Gene Goss to tell him of this conversation. Gene said he would tell Blue Diamond that our economic expert estimated the lifetime earning power of the fifteen miners to have been about eight hundred thousand dollars each, if they had lived, taking into account their salaries, expected increases in those salaries, probable promotions, and normal life expectancy. He would also warn Blue Diamond's counsel that, because of our successful appeal, Gene believed "the hawk is about to light." Still, when Blue Diamond called, they made no settlement offer, apparently because Blue Diamond was squabbling with its insurance counsel about how much money they would contribute to a proposed settlement.

# CHAPTER 12

# "The Ends of Justice"

The Sixth Circuit order had remanded our case to the United States District Court for the Eastern District of Kentucky "for trial." That did not leave any wiggle room, although I still was concerned about the last footnote of Judge Merritt's opinion. He and Judge Cecil had decided not to rule on Blue Diamond's "fifth alternative argument" to the Sixth Circuit that the "plaintiffs failed to establish the proximate cause of the explosion, and that the District Court should have granted Blue Diamond's motion for directed verdict on these grounds at the end of plaintiff's proof." Judges Merritt and Cecil held, "The District Court has not ruled on this question, and we do not believe consideration of this question at this time is proper." I feared this could allow Judge Hermansdorfer to commit further mischief. He might now decide the motion for a directed verdict that Blue Diamond had previously filed at the end of our curtailed first trial, rule that we had not established the proximate cause of the explosion during that earlier trial, deny us a new trial, and send us back for another appeal to the Sixth Circuit on the proximate cause issue.

But then I relaxed, assuming there could be no way Judge Hermansdorfer would not recuse himself from our case now that his coal holdings had become public. I should have known better. Judge Hermansdorfer called us to a status conference at his court in Catlettsburg, Kentucky, a small town near where he lived. At that hearing he gave no indication he might recuse himself. Instead he told us he might have to send us back to the Sixth Circuit for "clarification" of its remand order, and took all our numerous pending discovery motions "under advisement."

On the way out of his courtroom, I fortunately stopped in at the small clerk's office in Catlettsburg to arrange for another lawyer from my office, Gene Comey, to be allowed to appear with me in Judge Hermansdorfer's court in the future. We rarely had reason to be in the clerk's office in Catlettsburg, but while there I saw a public notice, on a small index card under the glass on the clerk's counter, which stated:

Please be advised that Judge Hermansdorfer has
leased the coal underlying his farm in Boyd County
to the Paul R. Coffey Construction Company for
strip mining purposes. If you feel this would make
any difference to you or your client, please make
your views known to Davis T. McGarvey, Chief
Clerk, United States District Court, Federal Building, Lexington, Kentucky, 40586 or to Judge Hermansdorfer.

This was the first and only notice from Judge Hermansdorfer pertaining to his coal holdings. I assumed he
now would claim, from this day forward, that everyone
had official notice of his coal holdings, because of this
small card in Catlettsburg. If we did not object now, we
might be waiving our right to have him removed from
our case. We could not risk another day before him. At
any moment he could order us back to the Sixth Circuit
and delay the new trial they had ordered.

On the airplane flight back to Washington we had a
layover in Pittsburgh. There I took out a draft motion to
recuse that I had been carrying around in my briefcase,
wondering if I would ever have to use it. Draped across
a few chairs in the terminal waiting room, I changed it
to a letter to Judge Hermansdorfer asking him to detail

on the public record all the facts relating to his coal holdings and coal royalties, so the plaintiffs could decide, based on a full record of the facts, whether to file a motion to recuse him. As soon as we filed this letter, Judge Hermansdorfer sealed it so the public would not know what we had asked. Bert Combs responded to our letter, and Judge Hermansdorfer sealed his response as well.

A few weeks later Judge Hermansdorfer wrote me a letter informing me that he would be transferring certain cases, including our case, for reassignment to other judges, because of his crowded docket. He added that in transferring our case he also gave "appropriate weight" to the "question of the appearance of partiality" we had raised, and that "the ends of justice are not well served by speculation as to the impartiality of any court."

A few days after that, we received a written order from Judge Hermansdorfer listing three cases in his court, with our case listed between the other two. His order stated that owing to his crowded docket of cases, he was transferring these three cases to the chief judge of the Court of Appeals for reassignment to another, less busy federal judge. This was a surprising decision, since Judge Hermansdorfer had been willing to take our case in the first place, despite his then busier criminal and civil docket, when Blue Diamond wanted to transfer our case from Tennessee to him. His real reason, of course, not stated in the public order, was to recuse himself from our case without saying so. I wondered what the lawyers in the other two cases thought when they learned their judge had so unexpectedly withdrawn from hearing their cases. Anyway, we were finally freed from Judge Hermansdorfer, though his order sealing the MESA report from publication still remained in effect. And he stayed on as the judge for the criminal cases against the Blue Diamond Coal Company and the Scotia Coal Company.

# CHAPTER 13

# A Wall of Evidence

For the next nine months we bounced around in limbo with no judge permanently assigned to our case. During that time, however, we were reminded how lucky we were to be out of Judge Hermansdorfer's court. The federal government had unwisely not moved to recuse Judge Hermansdorfer from the criminal cases against Blue Diamond and Scotia, even though the government now knew about his coal holdings. That left Judge Hermansdorfer free to issue a ruling which eviscerated the government's criminal cases. The judge agreed with Scotia, and its counsel Bert Combs, that the government could not use evidentiary records MESA had taken from Scotia's office without a warrant because their seizure violated Scotia's rights under the search and seizure clause of the Fourth Amendment. The criminal trial was postponed, and the government immediately appealed this decision to the Sixth Circuit.

During our nine months without a permanent judge,

we also learned that the Supreme Court had denied Blue Diamond's petition for certiorari. We were greatly relieved, even though we fully expected the Supreme Court would not hear an appeal from Judge Merritt's decision. But we still had no judge to move our litigation along to a new trial—until William O. Bertelsman was appointed by President Carter to fill a judicial seat newly created by Congress for the busy Eastern District of Kentucky. Judge Bertelsman was from Covington, Kentucky, across the river from Cincinnati, Ohio. He had an impeccable academic record, having graduated summa cum laude from Xavier College and first in his class at the University of Cincinnati College of Law. In his law practice he recently had been one of the plaintiffs' lawyers in one of the first mass class tort cases, the Beverly Hills Supper Club fire in Covington, Kentucky, which killed 165 people. He understood the plaintiff's side of a mass disaster lawsuit. As soon as Judge Bertelsman was confirmed to take his seat on the district court, he was assigned to our case. We could not have prayed for a better judge.

There would be no further delay. Judge Bertelsman immediately scheduled a pretrial conference that, unfortunately, conflicted with a ski vacation I had promised my wife and children. But a trial lawyer can never plan his or her life. He or she is at the whim of the court's calendar, and this first meeting with the judge was too important for me to ask the judge to reschedule it. My family went skiing and I flew to Kentucky to join the Scotia widows for our first appearance before Judge Bertelsman. At this pretrial conference, held coincidentally one month after Judge Hermansdorfer derailed the criminal cases against Blue Diamond and Scotia, Judge Bertelsman immediately ruled on the various longstanding motions Judge Hermansdorfer had "taken under advisement" in our civil case.

When Judge Bertelsman entered the court for that first day's hearing in our case, he immediately announced to all the lawyers present that his law clerk would now pass out his decisions on all the pending motions in this case. All of us were shocked to see how many decisions he had already made. One of his decisions allowed us to depose expert witnesses, including those involved in the MESA report. We would now be able to offer into evidence their expert opinions on the proximate cause of the explosion. His most surprising, and gratifying, decision was to schedule a trial date. He set aside three weeks for the trial to be held in Frankfort,

Kentucky, a neutral spot in the central part of the state, a long way from the coal fields of Eastern Kentucky. This protected us from Bert Combs's base of influence, although now we would be in the capital of Kentucky, where he had served four years as governor.

Things moved fast now. As we neared the trial date we hired jury experts to evaluate the local Frankfort jury pool. Frankfort is not a big city, so many of the jurors might be called from rural, agricultural areas outside the city. Their findings were disturbing, since those rural jurors did not think in big numbers. We learned that even a sympathetic jury in central Kentucky might not award more than one hundred thousand dollars per plaintiff. A leading plaintiff's lawyer in Frankfort thought the largest jury verdict we could hope for would be four hundred thousand dollars per plaintiff.

Judge Bertelsman also pushed both sides to settle the case. So I wrote a long letter to Bert Combs setting out our demands, which he immediately dismissed as too unrealistic for further discussion. He then tried to go behind my back to persuade Gene Goss to settle his two cases with Blue Diamond. When Gene said he would first have to talk with me, settlement talks ended.

Judge Bertelsman scheduled a final pretrial conference eleven days before the trial was to begin. The conference lasted almost all day, with Judge Bertelsman patiently doing what Judge Hermansdorfer never had done: ruling before the trial on the admissibility of one hundred ninety exhibits we planned to produce at the trial to prove Blue Diamond's direct involvement in causing the Scotia explosion. Judge Bertelsman agreed that we could offer numerous documents showing Blue Diamond's involvement in ventilation policy decisions for the Scotia mine, such as documents showing Blue Diamond's decision not to build new ventilation return airways needed at Scotia for at least four years before the explosion. He held this was admissible evidence to show Blue Diamond's recklessness for our punitive damages claim as well as to show Blue Diamond's control over Scotia's ventilation procedures.

We also offered numerous examples of Blue Diamond ventilation decisions at Scotia *after* the explosion. For example, Blue Diamond had hired an expert to determine what could be done in the future to ensure adequate ventilation to prevent another methane explosion at Scotia. The Federal Rules of Evidence provide that proof that someone fixes a problem after an accident occurs is admissible to show that that person had control over the problem before it occurred. So we argued that since Blue Diamond, rather than Scotia, hired this after-the-fact expert, that was proof of Blue Diamond's control of Scotia's ventilation requirements before the explosion. Blue Diamond's counsel vociferously objected. Judge Bertelsman agreed with us, "It's probative if you're the one who is supposed to correct the conditions."

We even offered evidence of Blue Diamond's decisions, after the explosion, regarding ventilation problems at the Upper Tygart mine at Scotia, a different mine from the mine where the explosion occurred. Judge Bertelsman told Blue Diamond's counsel, "It shows Blue Diamond getting into the details of ventilation problems, the very type of thing you say you didn't get into." He explained, "What you do afterward is relevant to show what you were doing before—to show control. . . . You are saying Blue Diamond never came in and got into these nitpicking decisions. He's trying to show . . . some examples where they did."

We also wanted to introduce the MESA report, or parts of it, even though MESA still had not published it. By this time Judge Hermansdorfer had ordered that MESA could publish its report, but "any publication of all or any part of said report shall contain the [following] notice":

Notice: This report is the subject of a pending action in the United States District Court for the Eastern District of Kentucky in the case of Blue Diamond Coal Company versus the Secretary of the Interior, et al. It has been adjudged in that action that there exists the appearances of agency impropriety which arguably affects the trustworthiness of this report. This report has been remanded to the Secretary for reconsideration.

Of course, MESA refused to publish a report with a notice that stated the report was arguably untrustworthy.

Nevertheless, Judge Bertelsman agreed with us that we should be allowed to use portions of the unpublished MESA report to show the basic facts our experts needed to prove the cause of the explosion. When Blue Diamond insisted that each document or page we offered from the MESA report had to have Judge Hermansdorfer's required notice, Judge Bertelsman adroitly decided that introduction into evidence of portions of the MESA report did not constitute "publication." So the jury would be allowed to see our MESA report exhibits without any notice that they might be untrustworthy.

We offered Mr. Bonnyman's handwritten notes that

future company policy would require that only "permissible equipment" be used everywhere in their gassy mines, even though the law still allowed certain "impermissible" equipment to be used in fresh air intake portals. Judge Bertelsman allowed that evidence because it "tends to show he got involved in these types of things." We also offered the mine ventilation map certified by a Blue Diamond engineer and given to MESA just before the explosion, the map that falsely showed ventilation stoppings still in place at the point where the explosion later occurred. Bert Combs had to admit the map was admissible, though he lamely argued that the failure to show that two essential concrete ventilation stoppings had been removed was just "an oversight."

I also wanted to introduce the minutes of Blue Diamond's operating department staff meetings, emblazoned with its motto "Higher Production—Lower Costs." Blue Diamond's lawyers tried to preclude these documents so I could not argue to the jury that "higher production" and "lower costs" recklessly led to unsafe mining practices. Judge Bertelsman responded, "I'd make the same argument if I was representing the plaintiffs." Blue Diamond argued that "Higher Production—Lower Costs" was prejudicial. Maybe so, said the judge, but he reminded Blue Diamond's counsel that the rule said such evidence was inadmissible only if it was "unfairly" prejudicial. This was not "unfair" prejudice, and Blue Diamond's counsel was free to argue to the jury their own interpretation of the meaning of "Higher Production—Lower Costs."

Judge Bertelsman understood that each document alone might not be enough to prove Blue Diamond control and thus liability. He explained that plaintiff's counsel "is talking about individual bricks where he's trying to build a wall. This is probative for what he's trying to prove. . . . He's trying to tilt the scale, to use another example, and I'm trying to decide what pebbles he can throw into the scale to tilt it."

I thought about the way my mentor, John Doar, helped prove President Nixon's direct involvement in all the details of Watergate, from the burglary to the coverup, by showing he nitpicked every decision at the White House, no matter how small. For example, Doar detailed how Nixon even insisted that he review the seating chart for every state dinner to be sure he agreed about where each person would be seated. Little pebbles like that tilted the scales enough so the public could more easily believe Nixon's complete involvement in every detail of Watergate.

Similarly, we were building our wall of evidence to

prove to the jury Blue Diamond's involvement in reck-lessly allowing methane to accumulate in the Scotia mine without proper ventilation. Finally, one of Blue Diamond's lawyers objected that our numerous exhibits were cumulative: "I suggest to Your Honor [that] after you've killed the rabbit you don't have to pick up a shovel and hit him fifteen times." Freud might say that this lawyer's choice of the number fifteen was interesting, since we were arguing that Blue Diamond had killed fifteen men.

I also requested that Bert Combs not be referred to as "Judge Combs" in front of the jury. Judge Bertelsman agreed. "Here we will just call everybody Mister and everybody will be equal. . . ." And he also ruled with us that Blue Diamond would not be able to tell the jury that some of the widows had remarried or that all of them had been receiving workers' compensation checks. Armed now with all these rulings, we were ready for our new trial on liability.

# CHAPTER 14

# "May God Forgive You . . . Because I Can't"

The prospect of the new trial prompted Judge Bertelsman to meet separately with each side to try to encourage a settlement. After we reduced our demand to one and a half million dollars for each woman, a total of twenty-two and a half million dollars, Judge Bertelsman leaned on Bert Combs: "What's your offer?" He replied, "Nothing."

Judge Bertelsman then told Bert Combs that, given the evidence he had seen, "a properly instructed jury could find that the evidence in this case would warrant a finding of liability against Blue Diamond Coal Company." He added that if the jury came in with an award of twenty-two and a half million dollars, as plaintiffs then were demanding, he would be hard-pressed to set it aside. After much back-and-forth, Bert Combs eventually raised his total offer to a "couple of million," we lowered our total demand to fifteen million dollars, they came up to four and a half million, and we countered with ten million. There we stalemated.

Almost on the eve of trial, Judge Bertelsman encouraged us once again to try to settle the case, so Bert Combs and I met again. In keeping with Kentucky's long history of horse racing, Mr. Combs told me I was gambling for a trifecta—I was trying to put three winning horses in a row across the line. He argued that we had to defeat a motion they intended to file asking the judge to direct a verdict in their favor; if we defeated that motion, we then had to overcome the Sixth Circuit's opinion holding that we had to prove Blue Diamond caused the Scotia explosion, separate and apart from anything done by the Scotia Coal Company or by Scotia's employees; and finally, if we won that, we still had to obtain a significant damage award from a jury in Frankfort, where Blue Diamond had a good shot at holding the verdict to no more than two to three hundred thousand dollars. I said we were willing to try. He warned me not to make the same mistake they had made in not settling with us earlier when they had a better chance at a low settlement.

Eventually we narrowed the gap between us, and finally they offered a total of six million dollars, which amounted to the four hundred thousand per family we had been told would be the best we could hope for in a trial. That was a lot more than the twenty-five thousand per family, a total of three hundred seventy-five thousand for all fifteen families, that Blue Diamond had offered on the eve of the oral argument before the Sixth Circuit. It looked as though the women's all-or-nothing gamble had paid off.

However, after talking with the women about this offer, I reported to Judge Bertelsman that they still wanted to go to trial. I told him they insisted they were not in this lawsuit only for money; they also wanted a trial to provide them their revenge against Blue Diamond. Judge Bertelsman told me to warn them that even if they won, which is never a certainty in a jury trial, the largest verdict they could expect would be about four hundred thousand dollars per family. He said he learned that from a lawyer in Frankfort, probably the same lawyer we had been talking to there. The judge urged me to persuade the women to accept the six-million-dollar offer.

Judge Bertelsman probably assumed the women, and I, were posturing so they could obtain a larger settlement, but I assured him they were serious. It was hard for them to agree to put a dollar figure on their husbands' lives, when they knew no amount of money would ever be the same as having them back. Geraldine McKnight said, "You cannot replace a man's life, what he might have accomplished or the difference he might have made in his children's lives." Unfortunately, however, all a court can do is exchange dollars for lives, a very cold trade. It was also hard for the women to end their fight with Blue Diamond, a fight which had brought them together and kept them together for the four years since the disaster.

It was difficult for me to let this case end as well. I had lived with the lawsuit and with these women for four years. We had grown very close to one another. We talked often in person and by phone as we traveled through each stage of the case, from the frustrations of so many delays, through the terrible disappointments when rulings went against us, to the highs when we won small and then larger victories. We were family. However, I also was concerned that they thought I could pull off miracles for them, having taken them from their desperate grief after their husbands' deaths, through the despair inflicted by Judge Hermansdorfer, to the joy of Judge Merritt's decision, to the utter luck of being assigned Judge Bertelsman. I worried that they wanted to see what pain I could inflict on Blue Diamond's managers in a fair trial, and I was afraid I could not fulfill their dreams of revenge.

Judge Bertelsman came up with an ingenious idea: to have the women and a high-ranking Blue Diamond officer come to his courtroom two days later, nine days before the trial. Judge Bertelsman would preside informally on a Saturday, without a court reporter, for a face-to-face meeting between the women and the Blue Diamond executive and its lawyers. This meant the women could tell these Blue Diamond representatives exactly how they felt, how Blue Diamond's reckless pursuit of more coal and money, in the face of an unsafe ventilation condition, had killed their husbands, destroyed their own lives and dreams, and left children who would never see their fathers again.

Five of the women agreed to represent all of the families at this high noon face-off. Blue Diamond sent someone other than Gordon Bonnyman. It was emotional and tearful. The women finally had their day in court, venting their anger and frustration on one of Blue Diamond's top officials. One woman put it this way: "Nobody on earth can put a price on what you took. You can't give us back our husbands. You can't give their daddies back to our kids. What do you see when you look in the mirror? How can you sleep at night? May God forgive you . . . because I can't." Another explained to the judge, "We want a settlement big enough to make them feel it costs more to kill a coal miner than to make sure he stays alive."

When they were through, we took a break. The Scotia widows now were ready to let their case end. If they were, so was I. They agreed to accept the six-million-dollar settlement, and Judge Bertelsman signed the settlement order two days before their new trial was to begin.

The women were relieved. Some had dreaded the idea of another trial. Libby Gibbs said, "I feel like we've been on trial ourselves. I just thank God it's over. I've been worried sick about going to court." All were happy they had been able to tell Blue Diamond's executive and lawyers how they felt. As Reda Turner said, "When we were in the judge's chambers, Blue Diamond's attorneys finally had to look us in the face. It was the first time in all these years they called us ladies and treated us with respect."

Although some of their fathers, still loyal to Scotia, had opposed their lawsuit, one father did tell them after their victory, "You women have made history." And they had. They had stood together against Big Daddy

Coal, and against those who gossiped about them and sniped at them, to win the largest per-person settlement ever obtained from a coal company in a coal mine disaster. Four hundred thousand dollars per family seems small by today's standards, but in 1980 in rural Frankfort, Kentucky, where their new trial was to take place, this was a great settlement. A federal judge in that area had recently voided an $812,000 jury verdict for the family of an eighteen-year-old employee negligently killed while at work. The judge held that the amount of the verdict "shocked his conscience" and ordered a new trial. That family had then settled for $400,000.

After the Scotia settlement was announced, I received a phone call from one of Blue Diamond's insurance counsels. He said, "You got one hell of a settlement. Very few lawyers would have taken that case, and even fewer would have persevered to the finish. You did a whale of a job for your clients, and a twenty-five-percent contingency fee is a very reasonable percentage." He "wanted to take a millionaire to lunch." Our law firm did earn a million dollars on this case.

# CHAPTER 15

# What Happened?

I t had taken more than four years to win the settlement
from Blue Diamond for the families of the fifteen men
who died in the first explosion at Scotia. But what happened to our efforts to obtain a settlement for the five
widows whose husbands died in the second Scotia explosion when they went into the mine, as volunteers
called for by MESA, to get the mine ready for the MESA
investigation?

We had been pressing the government to resolve that
litigation, which had been assigned to Judge G. Wix Unthank in Eastern Kentucky. Finally, within a year after
our settlement for the widows of the first Scotia explosion, the government agreed it was responsible for the
lives of those men killed in the second explosion and
agreed to settle with the five families we represented. We
had battled with the government for five years over ar-
cane issues involving "duty" and when you can and cannot sue the federal government. But we finally prevailed,

and the five families received $2.1 million dollars, about the same amount per family that the fifteen original Scotia widows had obtained.

What became of Judge Hermansdorfer? After recusing himself from the Scotia case, it would have been hard for him to preside over coal-related cases, which made up most of his docket, if litigants before him questioned whether he could be "like Caesar's wife . . . giving the appearance of being above reproach." He also had been blocked from reaching the United States Court of Appeals for the Sixth Circuit. Six months after the Scotia widows settled their lawsuit, Judge Hermansdorfer retired as a federal judge, citing severe back problems.

What about the criminal cases? Within a year after Judge Hermansdorfer retired from the bench, the Sixth Circuit reversed his decision that a warrantless search and seizure of statutorily required records from the office of a coal operator violates the Fourth Amendment. Then, years later, more than seven years after the Scotia mine explosion, and a week before its criminal trial, which also had been assigned to Judge Unthank, the Scotia Coal Company agreed to plead guilty to two criminal counts of the federal indictment. Scotia admitted it had failed to train each miner in the use of self-rescue equipment and had falsely reported that a preshift examiner, or fireboss, had checked the ventilation in the area on the date of the first explosion. It pleaded no contest to three other criminal counts.

Scotia's criminal penalty? A payment of sixty thousand dollars to four volunteer charities, which Scotia then deducted from its taxes. Blue Diamond's criminal penalty? All criminal charges were dropped against Blue Diamond as part of Scotia's plea bargain. As Harry Caudill, the lawyer and writer from Eastern Kentucky, said, "The Scotia situation reflects the complete inability of the United States to challenge culpable conduct. If I go out and run over someone with my car, I will be prosecuted, as I should be. If I negligently blow up a coal mine, nothing will be done." Nothing more than a mere sixty-thousand-dollar tax-deductible charitable contribution seven years later.

The Scotia widows moved on with their lives. Two went back to school and graduated from college, one becoming a teacher and one a librarian. One used the money to buy a house. Another was able to pay for expensive medical care for one of her children. One opened her own business in Harlan, Kentucky. One bought a long-haul truck and went into business as a truck driver. Half of the total settlement was set aside in annuities for the twenty-four children, with a large part of that to be paid to them after it had accumulated tax-free until their twenty-first birthdays. A number of those children now have graduated from college using those annuities, and have families of their own. The women also put aside large portions of their shares into annuities with guaranteed tax-free payments for twenty to thirty years. The cumulative total of the payments to the women and their children was about ten to twelve million dollars.

After the women received their first checks from the settlement, they invited me and the other lawyers from my firm and our wives to join them and Gene Goss for a celebration dinner in Harlan, Kentucky. The women presented me with a hand-sewn quilt, which I mounted on the wall in my office, and a silver cup, which sits on my desk, engraved GERALD M. STERN—THANK YOU FOR YOUR YEARS OF HARD WORK, PATIENCE AND FRIENDSHIP—THE SCOTIA WIDOWS. They now proudly called themselves the Scotia Widows.

# Epilogue

Why did the first Scotia mine explosion happen? Blue Diamond repeated its slogan at all managers' meetings: "Higher Production—Lower Costs." Driven to produce more and more coal out of the mine, and faster, while at the same time cutting costs, meant Blue Diamond did not stop to spend the time and money necessary to install the required ventilation controls before starting to mine coal in the new Two Left section. When Blue Diamond's lawyer tried to preclude me from arguing to the jury that "higher production" and "lower costs" recklessly led to unsafe mining practices, he claimed, "Nothing interferes more with production and cost at this mine than this explosion." I responded, "I wish you had thought of that earlier." Waiting a month or two in order to build the overcasts at the intersection of Two Southeast Mains and Two Left would have stopped production during that time in that one section, and temporarily raised Blue Diamond's costs, but certainly that would have been less expensive in the long run than the subsequent closing of the entire mine for almost a year, the damages they had to pay for the deaths of fifteen men, and the enormous legal fees and expenses they had to pay their lawyers to defend against our civil lawsuit and the government's criminal prosecution.

I also wish the Scotia managers and others in control had believed in and enforced the motto stamped on each heavy Scotia belt buckle: SAFETY PAYS. When it comes to safety, the mantra should be "Pay me now or pay me more later." In our lawsuit we proved that it is so much cheaper to pay for safety up front than to wait for the inevitable accident which costs even more to remedy later.

As we know, even thirty years after Scotia, coal miners still die because production and profits come before safety. This is an outrage, and unfortunately we will probably see even more coal miners die as our country turns more and more to our own coal reserves, instead of foreign oil, to fuel our economy. Nevertheless, some small legislative steps were taken after the recent onslaught of coal mine explosions in Utah, Kentucky, and West Virginia to force coal operators to make their mines safer. The Kentucky legislature required self-rescuers to last at least two hours rather than only one.

The Federal Mine Safety and Health Administration also issued emergency regulations to require mine operators to store additional breathing devices and other emergency supplies along escape routes. Some help, but not enough.

We still lag far behind on coal mine safety in this country. In Canada, mine operators are required to provide refuge stations in the mines—sealed-off areas with their own internal supply of oxygen lasting up to thirty-six hours, along with food and water. These safe rooms are credited with saving the lives of seventy potash miners in Western Canada recently when they were trapped underground for nearly twenty-four hours after a mine fire.

But legislation is not enough. Real change must come from the coal operators. When they cut corners on safety to mine more coal faster, they run the risk of explosions that may not only kill some of their miners, but also require the closure of their mines and the cessation of all coal production. That happened at Scotia for 235 days, and more recently at the Crandall Canyon mine, closing it forever. When the Crandall Canyon mine was permanently sealed, its owner said, "I'll never go near that mountain again."

## EPILOGUE

When coal mine operators really believe "safety pays"—that it is cheaper to operate safely, even if safety cuts into production and profits in the short run—then underground coal mining will become safer, and a trapped miner may never again have to scribble a dying note to a loved one: "Oh God for one more breath."

# Acknowledgments

I thank:

The Scotia Widows, whose names are listed in the dedication, for welcoming me into their lives and allowing me to represent them. They helped me to learn patience and persistence in the pursuit of what is right.

The Rogovin, Stern and Huge lawyers George Frampton, Jonathan Schiller, Gene Comey, and Ellen Silverman, who worked many long hours on behalf of the women; our firm's paralegal, Rob McDuff; and all the members of our firm who charged billable hours to keep the firm financially successful while I was off fighting for a cause that could have yielded our firm little or no remuneration at so many stages of the case.

Gene Goss, our local lawyer in Harlan, Kentucky, whose common sense and keen intelligence guided me through many difficult days.

Bill Bishop and Tom Bethell, journalists who shone

a light on the dark corners of Eastern Kentucky so all of us could see the need for justice.

Tom Galloway and Davit McAteer, warriors for the coal mining families of West Virginia and Kentucky, who first brought my name to the attention of Dan Hendrickson and Sally Maggard.

Dan Hendrickson and Sally Maggard, volunteers whose sense of moral necessity brought me and others into the fray and kept the Scotia Widows united in their long struggle.

Judges Gilbert Merritt and William O. Bertelsman, outstanding, sympathetic public servants who represent our judiciary at its finest.

My agent, Robert Lescher, and my editor, Robert Loomis, who once again have made it possible for me to tell the world about the good people of Appalachia. I can never repay them for their guidance and support in publishing *The Buffalo Creek Disaster* and now this book.

My son, Dr. Eric Stern, and my friend, Alan Friedman, for reading and rereading drafts of this book and providing me with invaluable comments, criticism, and encouragement.

Finally, I thank my soulmate and lifelong companion, my wife, Linda, to whom this book is also dedicated, for her constant love and support. She had to live through my physical absences during the litigation in Kentucky many years ago, and now she has had to live through my mental absences as I buried myself and my thoughts in the writing of this story. Thank you for understanding.

## ABOUT THE AUTHOR

Gerald M. Stern was a founding partner of the Washington, D.C., law firm of Rogovin, Stern and Huge. Prior to that he was a partner with Arnold and Porter for eleven years, where he was the lead counsel for the survivors of the Buffalo Creek coal mining disaster in West Virginia. He wrote about that experience in *The Buffalo Creek Disaster,* a recently reissued book still widely used in law schools. Before joining Arnold and Porter he was a trial attorney with the Civil Rights Division of the United States Department of Justice, trying voting discrimination cases in the South. He wrote about those experiences in two books, *Southern Justice* and *Outside the Law.* He has also served as general counsel of Occidental Petroleum Corporation and as special counsel to the United States Department of Justice. Presently, he is a legal consultant and lives in Washington, D.C.